Democracy, Chaos, and the New School Order

For
Richard L. Hansen
H. L. Richards High School
Oak Lawn, Illinois
Inspiring teacher and friend

Democracy, Chaos, and the New School Order

Spencer J. Maxcy

CORWIN PRESS, INC.
A Sage Publications Company
Thousand Oaks, California 91320

For information, address:

Corwin Press, Inc.
A Sage Publications Company
2455 Teller Road
Thousand Oaks, California 91320

SAGE Publications Ltd.
6 Bonhill Street
London EC2A 4PU
United Kingdom

SAGE Publications India Pvt. Ltd.
M-32 Market
Greater Kailash I
New Delhi 110 048 India

Printed in the United States of America

Library of Congress Cataloging-in-Publication Data

Maxcy, Spencer J.
   Democracy, chaos, and the new school order / Spencer J. Maxcy.
      p. cm.
   Includes bibliographical references and index.
   ISBN 0-8039-6198-7 (cl. : alk. paper).—ISBN 0-8039-6199-5 (pbk. :
alk. paper)
   1. Education—United States. 2. Educational change—United
States. 3. School management and organization—United States.
I. Title.
LA217.2.M39 1995
370'.973—dc20   94-23544

This book is printed on acid-free paper.

95 96 97 98 99 10 9 8 7 6 5 4 3 2 1

Production Editor: Yvonne Könneker
Ventura Typesetter: Danielle Dillahunt

Contents

Preface

The Problem of School Restructuring

There is a vast and pervasive effort to reform public schools going on in the United States today. Called by names such as school restructuring, educational decentralization, educational redesign, and site-based management, these reform efforts have a number of characteristics in common. Reformers see educational systems to be too bureaucratic and centralized for their own good. Educational systems have become unmanageable, critics argue, because their fundamental structures are out-of-date. School leaders have lost touch with the communities they were to serve. Reformers therefore propose to restructure educational organizations. They wish to return control to the local communities. Parents, teachers, and citizens in general are being empowered to take over decision making. Traditional management is giving way to teams and work groups. Centralized school bureaucracies are being replaced by local school councils (LSCs) in state after state. Fiscal responsibility is being relocated to smaller, more local school units. School councils select the principal and teachers. Restructurers are now exercising whatever authority is required to give the schools back to those closest to the educational task.

By the year 2002 every Alabama public school will have implemented school-based decision making. Local school councils will take charge of the day-to-day management of each and every school in the state. Central office bureaucracy is under attack. Kentucky has passed statewide restructuring legislation called the Kentucky Educational Reform Act (KERA; see Kentucky Department of Education, 1990), enacting many of the same reforms. Urban school systems such as Chicago, Miami, and New York City have launched decentralizing efforts that divide the metropolis into small units, each autonomous from the historically inefficient central office.

The American schools are passing through a wrenching period of reorganization as they confront one of the worst periods our nation has faced in its history. By all accounts, the social forces bearing down on the schools are one reason why school reforms have been touted so highly as solutions. Crime and violence, AIDS, poverty, unemployment, and a host of related social problems have entered the schools. The American culture is in a state of extreme and turbulent adolescence. Some writers label this crisis of culture *chaos*. Critical and quite real problems plague all those who are involved with schooling—teachers, parents, administrators, and children. The terrible harm that can befall a youngster attending any one of our institutions is alarming. Although only a few decades ago chewing gum was considered a serious infraction, now schools are scenes of shootings, drug overdoses, and rapes.

Despite the flurry of new school organizational forms, the programs proposed and enacted are surprisingly conventional. There is a strange absence of inspiration in the designs for school reorganization advanced to date. Schemes for school reconfiguration seem to lack moral purpose and heart. Critics of the movement point to the intractable nature of the American educational bureaucracy, the resistance of teacher unions, an entrenched administration, and the overwhelming threat of external pressure groups to change schools into self-serving enterprises. Perhaps we have asked too much of our more than 2 million educators when we tell them to embrace yet another reform (Archbald, 1993).

Whenever the United States has felt threatened, the schools have been kneaded into frontline institutions of response. During World War II, school children made up boxes of bandages, soap, and other supplies to be sent to American troops fighting the Nazis. The postwar period found schools teaching civil defense courses, their hallways converted into fallout shelters for nuclear attack. The Russian *Sputnik* in the 1950s prompted American educational bureaucrats to shift to curricula heavy in science and math. In the 1960s and 1970s perceived economic crises prompted schools to offer classes in career education and free enterprise to adjust children to the "world of work." In the 1980s competition from Japan pushed educational reformers to embrace the notion of "effective education" to regain market share.

It is not surprising that contemporary social problems of all sorts should prompt reformers once again to focus on schools to fight the threatening forces perceived. Whenever Americans have become overwhelmed by a sense of impending social evil, they have fastened on the schools to meet the attack. The present-day chaos has prompted a similar response to external threat. However, what is unique about the present reform effort is the emphasis placed not on curriculum for competition but rather on organizational size as the major culprit. The fundamental challenge is how to organize schools so that the potential for good overshadows that of harm. The interesting features of present-day reforms are their move away from castigating the teacher, the student, or the parent and their almost insidious desire to place the blame for America's incapacitation in meeting the threats of crime, disease, and national economic competition on schools as forms of organization.

Scholars and researchers today have sidestepped the historical search for causes and have concentrated their firepower not on the agents and forces but instead on the administrative mind-set that has governed public schools since the days of Horace Mann. It is assumed that the institution of the public school has degenerated from an ordered and rational system into a galactic chaos, incapable of responding to the needs it was designed to fulfill. Teachers and parents wring their hands and lament the lack of voice. Academics in universities around the country debate the conditions and the cures. Few of us as parents or patient observers are free from our personal views on the subject of school reform in the face of such difficulties.

Contributors to the controversy over what shape our new schools shall take cluster into several groups: First, some organizational theorists (the social scientists) propose to conceptualize the school and study its operations with an eye to transforming the educational system into a superior device for delivering educational outcomes and shaping learner products. These researchers and academics often differ as to what the school as an organization is, how it is to be examined, and what we should do with the findings from such research. Nonetheless, they are committed to the scientific and rational study of the problems of schools as structured systems in society and retain a faith in modern social life as the best environment for efficient and effective schooling.

A second set of reformers (accountants-clerics) propose certain restructuring, reconfiguration, and streamlining of schools so that student learning may be more efficiently delivered. Upset by the waste of money and lack of moral-ethical virtues found in schools, these reformers have written popular magazine articles and books advocating restructuring. Proposals as to how this shall be accomplished vary widely, from making public schools competitive marketplaces for students to privatizing education entirely. These reformers speak of charter schools and vouchers as the means for educational renewal. This collection of reformers is made up of policy analysts, school board members, government educational bureaucrats, and academics who view schools as modifiable organizations that must be fine-tuned over time. Within this group are individuals who wish to reform schools along moral-ethical lines but always in terms of time-tested standards and ideals. Elitist and strong believers in a social Darwinist universe, advocates preach competition and character fitness. The agenda for this constituency is highlighted by a call for teaching educational virtues, embracing a national curricula, and testing schools and teachers against international standards of institutional effects.

A third group of reformers (destructurers) propose that schools and American society are victimizing children and reproducing the worst features of society. These reformers favor nothing less than the overthrow of conventional educational forms and processes. Nearing anarchy, the group favors local control of education, empowerment of teachers and parents, and the dissolution of the state and local educational bureaucracies. Rather than restructure, these reforms seek a destructuring of the massive bureaucracy of public schooling in the United States. Romantics through and through, these reformers seem to harken back to the free school movement of the 1960s. Small-scale and local in nature, the new schools are to be purged of professional administrators and run by parents. Free from the purse strings of state and district educational bureaucracies, such enterprises would be sensitive and humane sites for educating children and youth.

These three groups are not easy to label as either liberal or conservative. The members may adopt parts of each other's stances and attempt to operationalize an eclectic reform package. There are no hard-and-fast lines drawn between the advocates here. Parents, teachers, and students may well be silent in the face of these arguments and activities of the major players in the drama over schooling.

Although each of these groups plies its arguments for school restructure, the historical players in education counterattack. School boards and their professional associations resist school reorganization because such moves threaten their vested interests in educational governance. Many school boards and members are likely to be out of jobs. They argue that local school management placed in the hands of principals, teachers, and parents will cause long-running problems for effective school management. Certain factions blanch at any proposals for change: What was good enough for our fathers is good enough for our children!

Professional school people may also resist arguments for school reordering. School administrators, professors of educational administration, and some professional administrator organizations are cautious critics of school reorganization reforms. Nurtured in the belief that schools are structures to be managed rationally, this mentality finds the decentralization and democratization of school leadership to be a threat to educational administration as a profession. Such critics assert that expertise is not to be sacrificed to management by committee. The field of educational administration has been under the gun to reform its school principal preparation programs for years, and only recently have such changes begun in some of the universities (Murphy, 1993; Quantz & McCabe, 1991). However, the field of educational administration by and large is resistant to teachers or parents assuming leadership positions in which the school administrators have traditionally held sway.

Nonetheless, the groundswell for change has convinced all of these groups that school reform is currently a serious business. They all agree that the schools in the United States are going to look quite different in the 21st century. What the new schools will be like and how they will be governed are the essentially contested issues of the reform effort now under way.

This book presents quite a different take on the reforms aimed at our nation's schools. It proposes that school restructuring has fallen on hard times and that the controversy has heated up because of certain embedded assumptions about public school organization and our times. I suggest the adoption of a *critical pragmatic* approach to the problems of educational change. My principal thesis is that we need such an overarching philosophy of culture and life if we are to make sense of the postindustrial society we inhabit. The chapters that follow examine a number of issues pertinent to school restructuring through this critical pragmatic lens: issues of research philosophy, the chaotic versus orderly nature of culture and society, the role of politics in school organization, the shift from a modern to a postmodern world, the virtue of educational reconstruction versus restructure, and the part values are to play in the new school order. The end-in-view is shown to be nothing less than a transformation of notions of how postliberal political culture and schooling are to be conceptualized and what this reconstructed vision may say about educational leadership in the next century.

School restructuring is taken to be a problem. In the face of the rhetoric of restructure and reorganization, this text offers a discourse highlighting reconstruction of schools into beautiful sites for richly composed and purposeful living. The position of the school leader as bureaucrat is replaced by that of a collective transactional leadership. The educational landscape shifts from factory to an aesthetically rich moral-ethical garden. The concept of school as organization moves from the metaphor of chaotic machine system to democratic, pluralistic, and discursive community. This book seeks to reposition grassroots democracy as the essential ground on which to rebuild public education in the United States.

Design of the Text

This text has been formed to help the participants and interested observers of the school restructuring controversy to understand both the nature of school reform and the intelligent means available for guiding changes leading to better schools for our children and youth. There are no lists or formulas offered, and no patent programs will be touted. Simple depictions of and palliatives for the problems besetting our school organizations have been part of the reason why school restructuring has been lackluster to date. Ultimately, this book is theoretical and philosophical, if for no other reason than that the problems discussed are not simple nor are the suggested remedies easy.

This text fits into a genre that may be termed *educational criticism* but is unique in the version of pragmatic thinking employed, the emphasis on our postmodern condition, and the attention given to a new postliberal political climate. The normative recommendation is for school reconstruction rather than for school restructuring. The following chapters are aimed at uncovering the mystery of schools seen as organizations, because it is at the level of collective and group effort that the promise of public education has been hampered so seriously. I believe that any informed participant in schooling in the United States will be able to follow my diagnoses and prescriptions for successful educational redesign. It is anticipated that readers will be teachers, parents, and school administrators, as well as scholars in the fields of foundations of education, curriculum theory, and educational leadership and administration.

Subsequent chapters will touch on some of the panoply of existing theories, plans, reports, and assessments of new directions in the reform of schools seen as organizations. However, my interest is not in the detailed analysis of failed restructuring; rather, I am after nothing short of a completely new way of thinking about education. To some degree the answer to education queries lies in history. Historical roots for contemporary restructuring will be examined against the backdrop of theories of chaos and order. The central task is to offer a set of considerations—a meliorism—loosely termed critical and pragmatic, by which such plans and prospects may be judged and tested. As part of this middle-range set of intellectual moves, I shall make a plea to introduce a neglected posture toward schools for a new postmodern era. This book will seek to provide a democratic and moral-ethical model for the reconstruction of certain features of democratic social life and to lay them against proposals to reconstruct public education.

Through a critical and pragmatic analysis of contemporary calls for restructuring schools, I shall show both the problem and the methods by which resolutions may be generated. This text is aimed at intellectual surgery: I wish to reattach a reflective and practical organ in order to better grasp essentially contested issues facing schooling at this most crucial point in our national development. The strategy of "practical judgment" is encouraged as the discourse about school restructuring moves forward. The principal belief fueling this enterprise is that in the rush to do something quick to fix the schools, we have overlooked the democratic base on which free public schools operate while simultaneously jettisoning the methods of pragmatic intelligence so useful in such confusing social settings. This book is directed at producing a clear set of procedural values and fundamental enabling beliefs to aid in the redirection of school reform.

This book seeks to address a great void in the conversations regarding school reform. Little has been said of the timbre of the discourse and its tie with the rhythm of guided action. Little has been mentioned of the need to approach schools as we approach the most beautiful parts of our lives. We have, in short, seriously underdetermined our discourse from an artistic point of view. I seek to reintroduce shape, color, and voice to conversations about schools as constructed sites of life development. My remarks shall stand in sharp contrast to the positivist engineering language with its lexicon of bureaucratic speech. In the place of restructuring I shall propose reconstruction of schooling. Instead of 18th-century philosophical Enlightenment rationality, a critical and pragmatic philosophy will be introduced. Rather than conceiving of culture as modern and technological, this book examines the postmodern and posttechnical elements emerging in our lives. Instead of a chaos of hidden precision and control, I explore the concepts of chance and coherence. In the place of a democracy of elites, this book entertains a truly participatory, culturally pluralistic, and discursive democracy for schools. Last, in the place of compassion and caring, I show our moral, ethical, religious and other values requiring an artistic and naturalized mentality that helps reevaluate school organizations as sites of learning and growth.

Since the 5th century B.C. and the writing of Plato, scholars have been aware of the argument that at their best, schools must make honest and beautiful children. We have lost significant allegiance to this aim. Through a type of archaeology of organizational life, this text will seek to resurrect the first and most significant purpose for which schools were created and have been organized.

General Plan of the Book

In the pages that follow, contemporary proposals to reconfigure schools will be examined using a pragmatic approach. There is a renaissance in pragmatism going on in which a new relevance of thought to action is emerging, with emphasis on antifoundational epistemology, experimental and reflective thinking, and attention to practical consequences. Cultural critique has taken on a new value in the efforts of scholars to address the marginalized and heretofore untapped voices that may inform new societal configurations. How shall we organize our social institutions, and to what end?—this is the problematic I shall engage in the pages that follow.

In Chapter 1 the essential tension in theorizing about schools as organizations is outlined. Beneath efforts to reorganize schools has been a fundamental and underlying set of assumptions regarding the nature and development of schools as organizations. The task of the first chapter is one of illustrating how it is that we are in the present quandary relative to school reform, how the frameworks approach to the study of institutions is faulty, as well as how a nonfoundational notion of organizational inquiry improves on the faults of traditional social science methodological assumptions.

Chapter 2 explores the question of whether or not social organizations such as schools are chaotic. The general popularity of chaos theory in physics and natural science in particular and efforts to extrapolate this viewpoint to educational descriptions is challenged. This chapter discusses the historical and logical reasons for chaos versus order polarized thinking in Western society and seeks to critique the application of overly abstract characterizations in the form of grand theories to the practice of teaching and learning in educational institutions.

Chapter 3 discusses the appropriateness of democratic models for school organizations in developed and developing nations. I argue here that democracy as a form of social living has been underutilized in democratic nations largely because of a theoretical misunderstanding. The nature of this misappropriation and the corrective for it are laid out in this chapter.

Chapter 4 examines three efforts to restructure schools in Kentucky, Chicago, and West Feliciana (Louisiana). These proposals are tested first against a modernist model of interrogation and then against a postmodern, critical pragmatic model for educational reform. The virtues of the latter approach will be highlighted.

In Chapter 5 I explore the pluralistic nature of democracies and raise the question of individual autonomy relative to contemporary fractured democratic states. I argue here that pluralism functions in at least two ways: descriptively and normatively. Three kinds of democratically based pluralistic recommendations are examined, with the best option highlighted and applied to the problem of school reordering in the future.

Chapter 6 argues that schools are buoys in a moral sea, that schools in a democratic society must rest on aesthetic and moral-ethical processes, and that heretofore the failure of restructuring efforts in schooling in the United States has resulted from reformers overlooking the polyvalue basis of all patterned social life.

Chapter 7 concludes this text by offering possible guides for the reconstruction of school organizations for the 21st century.

These chapters review the theories of organization, the conception of schools as organized chaos, and the role of the individual and the group vis-à-vis organized experiences. I examine democracy as informing several possible organizational schemes for educational institutions, the role of social and cultural knowledge and school organization, cultural pluralism, and educational organization. In addition, this book explores the historical record of efforts to reconstruct school organizations and the role of art, morals, ethics, and values in reconstructing schools as social spaces.

My goal in writing this text is to provide policy makers, parents, teachers, school administrators, and academics a set of springboards for more successful school reform. It is assumed throughout this book that sound ideas make for fruitful practice. Without artfully designed schools we shall not succeed in the postmodern era in our task of providing the best educational experiences for our children. I hope that the views expressed in these pages will be helpful in our efforts to make beautiful and successful people for the new millennium.

Acknowledgments

I wish to thank my wife, Doreen, for carefully editing the many drafts of this book. We met over a "Dewey paper" more than 20 years ago, and she continues to inspire me with her love and kindness. Thanks to my two children—my daughter, Colleen, and son, Spence—for checking sources and accompanying me on many trips through the dusty stacks of libraries.

The present text is the richer for "botanizing expeditions" with James Scheurich at the University of Texas at Austin. Jackie Blount of Iowa State University and Colleen Capper of the University of Wisconsin at Madison sensitized me to the feminist and minority criticisms of educational organization and administration. Postmodern and chaos dialogues with Bill Doll and Margaret Sullivan of Louisiana State University (LSU) stimulated my rethinking the appropriateness of this set of theories for organizational theory. Jim Garvin, Dianne Taylor, and Richard Fossey, also of LSU, helped in reconceptualizing school restructuring as a movement. Abbas Tashakkori aided my understanding of Hispanic minority interests in education. I am also clearer on the notions of democracy and research methodology because of talks with Bill Johnston, Bob

Slater, Chuck Fazzaro, Lou Miron, Fen English, Betty Steffy, Joe Green, Bill Greenfield, and Wayne Parent. A special expression of thanks to Jim Garrison, Gary Anderson, and William Foster who read early drafts and provided kind criticisms. Although I am indebted to all of these colleagues, I take full responsibility for my renderings here.

Chapter 5 began as a lecture before the faculty of the Division of Education at the University of Texas at San Antonio, made possible by an invitation from Ray Calabrese and Chris Borman. Chapter 6 grew from my response to a set of papers presented at the American Educational Research Association conference in Atlanta in April 1993. I am indebted to the participants, Catherine Marshall, George Noblit, Lynn Beck, Emilie Siddle Walker, and to those attending this session for stimulating my thinking on caring and its role in educational reorganization.

Kofi Lomotey offered advice and counsel on many technical facets of production for which I am in his debt. The LSU School of Design librarian, Sandra Mooney, was most helpful in locating scarce sources for this project. I am grateful as well to my students for the many class discussions that only improved the present effort. Thanks to Gathago Murkuria and Elizabeth Arceneaux for research assistance. And finally, I wish to express my appreciation to my editors, Alice Foster and Yvonne Könneker, for making my rough ideas into the final aesthetic form you hold in your hands.

About the Author

Spencer J. Maxcy is Professor of Education in the Department of Educational Administrative and Foundational Services at Louisiana State University in Baton Rouge. He has written extensively on schooling and culture. His recent books pertinent to leadership and organizations are *Educational Leadership: A Critical Pragmatic Perspective* and *Postmodern School Leadership: Meeting the Crisis in Educational Administration.*

1

𝕾

How Did the
Schools Get This Way?

Nations around the world are experiencing a democratizing process that was unheard of less than a decade ago (Fukuyama, 1992). Institutions within these democratizing nations are also experiencing rapid changes in their structure and operations. In the name of school restructuring, school reformers in the United States are setting the tone for worldwide educational change by moving from large bureaucratic educational systems to small-scale autonomous schools. In conjunction with these structural changes, certain realignments of function have emerged: empowering teachers and parents in the decision-making processes of school governance, rethinking the missions of schooling, and reassessing curriculum and teaching methods (Hess, 1991).

Although proposals for changes in school structure and operation should be interrogated by asking how such shifts in organizational character are warranted in terms of changing political and cultural conditions, quite different sources of support are offered. Educational reform arguments increasingly are grounded on the bedrock of research. Hence, it is within the field of educational research—particularly research and theory of school organization—that we must look for the reasons why school restructuring is faltering today.

Frameworks, paradigms, and other architectures for conceiving of the object of the research enterprise need to be examined. The relativism and absolutism informing such metaphors must be surfaced. In short, we must understand how school restructuralists are able to talk the way they do about what schools are and what they ought to become.

The concern for engaging in a kind of archaeology of educational organizational research methodology becomes even more vital when considering the postmodern cultural changes that Americans are witnessing. Democratization and the emergence of new postliberal political movements are gaining support around the globe. Change in modes of associated learning and living are under way. Structuralist research with its metaphors of framework and pattern needs to be replaced by a more richly textured philosophy of a critical and pragmatic type in order to design better schools in the future.

Frameworks of Organization

Restructuring talk in educational circles is tightly aligned, albeit implicitly, with certain key historical theories and vocabularies of organization. Americans have only recently come to take seriously the meanings that *organization* and *structure* have relative to schools. The science of educational administration had its beginnings in the early part of 20th century and has flourished in only a few Western nations such as the United States, Canada, and Australia.

The current rhetoric surrounding school reorganization is fueled by experts in the social sciences. Nearly all of the studies of school structure are cast in sociological, psychological, political science, or public administration vocabularies. Terms and phrases such as *motivation, efficiency, effectiveness, outcomes-based, learning products,* and so forth provide a lexicon for theories aimed at control and management but leave on the margins any discourse revolving around moral and aesthetic concepts. Such terms and phrases are hooked on scaffolds of an intellectual sort. Frameworks, models, and other abstract linguistic representations are constructed to simplify the inquiry process and make it more dramatic. A profound assumption underwriting some social science research scholarship is the belief, historically reported, that social organizations have been studied from differing structured theoretical perspectives (frameworks) and should be capable of being so studied in the future.

The history of education has depicted schools as either a series of organizational forms (Callahan, 1962) or, as Tyack (1974) noted, "the One Best System" (p. 8). Modern views of organization grew from the moment when humans no longer took themselves to be mirrored reflections of God and nature and began theorizing on the basis of human action emerging from reasoned discourse. The Enlightenment vision of humans was one of ceasing to depend on external authority as the root and branch of belief (Toulmin, 1990).

Following Kuhn (1962/1970), Bolman and Deal (1991), Burrell and Morgan (1979), and Morgan (1986) all have proposed that it is possible to study social behaviors within differing and distinct *frameworks*, or *paradigms*. A framework is a research routine, a structured series of questions about the situation under investigation, the steps to be taken, the type and location of data to be uncovered, and the means to be used to process the data and specify the results (Diesing, 1991). The frame also entails certain assumptions regarding what is real, what is true, what is of value, and what is the appropriate method for discovery (Burrell & Morgan, 1979). The latter presumed matters are not verifiable by the frame but rather stand as types of ideal standards for determining framework success. For the purposes of this inquiry into contemporary school reform, I examine the following four popular frames used in the research on school organizations, display their character and contents, and attempt to reveal their faults.

Scientific Framework

The scientific study of organizations began in the United States around 1900 under the influence of the work of Frederick Taylor (1911) and Henri Fayol (1949). Efforts to improve industrial efficiency led Taylor and his followers to develop strategies for measuring factory tasks and streamlining production. Scientific management spread to the schools through the work of W. W. Charters (1925). The aim became one of measuring efficiency and manufacture of "school products" (children).

In the 1930s this efficiency approach was replaced by the human relations approach growing from the work of Mayo (1933) and Roethlisberger and Dickson (1939)—the General Electric study—and the writings of Mary Parker Follett (1924, 1942). In the late 1930s and early 1940s, Chester Barnard (1938) and Herbert Simon (1947/1965), using the behavioral science approach, sought to provide scientific specifications of managerial behaviors. This work significantly influenced the school administration researchers, and a number of writings emerged dealing with school leadership viewed as human behavior.

After 1940 the systems approach emerged in several forms. One version of systems thinking influencing school administration research was the theory movement, which sought to derive theories of educational administration based on data sets. Evers and Lakomski (1991) called another the new orthodoxy, best represented in the work of Hoy and Miskel, *Educational Administration: Theory, Research, and Practice* (1991), which characterized schools as open systems. Last, chaos theory forms another version of the systems framework. This theory holds the assumption that the nature of the organizational reality is not orderly but disorderly. Chaos thinkers looking at school organizations argue that their fundamental nature is one of extreme complexity. The role of the researcher is to penetrate this chaos using nonlinear management techniques and to locate the emerging new patterns within (Priesmeyer, 1992).

These differing researchers and approaches seemed to share a fundamental belief in science and the methods of observation, data collection, testing, and so forth in determining the truth about the real world of schools. Morgan (1986) found certain strengths in this framework. These researchers had as their major focus the tasks and, more specifically, the behaviors of administrators. They sought to specify the decision-making procedures utilized and their relationship to organizational goals. The entire vision was one of a potentially discursive state of affairs.

Given this first framework or metaphorical approach, educational organizations are subject to rational understanding and linguistic depiction. The logical and epistemological features of the characterizations of such organizations match perfectly with the real structures humans inhabit. Rendering true accounts of such organizations is not only possible, it is inevitable. We are led to believe that a science of school organizations is within our grasp.

The scientific framework has been labeled "positivist" and suffers from the disadvantages identified with this movement in science and the social sciences. From the first positivist, Auguste Comte, to the logical positivists, the preference for sanitized language and logical rigor has blindsided social scientists into believing that what is largely a matter of satisfying narrow professional norms is "value-free research."

Although Dewey (1938) has been criticized for scientizing the study of social life, he argued that inquiry into human collective life requires much more than the formalized procedures of laboratory science (although the attitudes of science were not deemed harmful). Instead of marketing philosophy as a superscience, corrective of laboratory technique, Rorty (1979) emphasized narratives and poetry, novels and stories—all as illuminative of the nature of human public and private life.

Where the scientific framework assumes that the interplay between concepts specified linguistically as variables matches point for point the interstices of human interaction in the life world, we have fallen heir to the fallacy of linguistic idealism. It is not far from assuming the reality of numbers (numerology) and then postulating public policy based on this metaphysics.

Something of a controversy was generated by a series of articles and books that sought to challenge or redefine this positivist approach in educational research (Aper & Garrison, 1989; Bredo, 1989; Eisner, 1988; J. Maxwell, 1992; N. Maxwell, 1984; Phillips, 1987). Although a large number of sources seem to see positivism as moribund, it continues to dominate research activities: The patient may be dead, but no one has informed the surviving kin. A growing number of authors have suggested that we move beyond both quantitative and qualitative research techniques (and the warrants for these) to embrace a postpositivist, poststructuralist, or postmodernist approach to inquiry (Bernstein, 1983; Maxcy, 1994; Popkewitz, 1984; Scheurich, 1994).

Interpretivist Framework

For want of a better, more inclusive category, it is possible to characterize a second set of research orientations toward school organizations as interpretivist. The interpretivist researcher sees the social world in unstable (sometimes chaotic) condition. Social reality is seen best from the inside, as a participant. Objectivity is a myth. Unlike the social and behavioral science approach that positions the researcher outside the phenomena under study, this insider approach seeks to delve deeply into the inner state of characters and events within organizations. Naturalistic inquiry, phenomenological research, and cultural and social investigation are just some of the versions of this basic approach.

Theorists in educational administration who abide by this research orientation see organizations as essentially socially constructed realities. Organizations exist only in the perceptions of human beings as subjective individuals engaged in the generation of meanings. Researchers are pledged to the study of expressions of subjectivity in the form of language, beliefs, myths, and rituals. In organizational settings, viewed as cultures or microsocieties, researchers try to determine how subjects interpret situations and to understand their actions. The effort of the investigator is to see how these interpretations grow from the subjects' reasons, motives, and intentions.

The strength of this interpretivist approach for the study of educational organizations lies in the assumption, at least partially correct, that school people are dramatically shaped by their beliefs. Schools, viewed as cultures, are taken to be arenas in which more than simple goal seeking is involved. The subjective understanding of the school is far more important than the external structural features examined by the scientific researchers.

The disadvantage of the interpretivist framework lies in its ignoring the role of conflict and contention in organizational life. Domination, repression, control, and other devices of imposed order are not significant for advocates of this research approach. The essentially political nature of organizational life is unspecified. There is no real interest in reform (Burrell & Morgan, 1979). This heightened sensitivity to the administrator's, teacher's, and student's own perceptions of reality lead to the consideration of yet another framework.

Radical Framework

Burrell and Morgan (1979) found members of this group committed to "change, emancipation, and potentiality in an analysis which emphasizes structural conflict, modes of domination, contradiction, and deprivation" (p. 79). Education theorists influenced by this framework typically take educational organizations to be arenas of conflict. In the hands of Foster (1986) and Bates (1980), educational administration is seen as perpetuating inequality. This frame shares with the interpretivist paradigm a belief in the socially constructed nature of reality. Committed to the virtue of critique, advocates argue that domination of one group over another in school situations perpetuates ("reproduces") an exploitation condition in the society at large. One class or one segment of society comes to dominate others (Bourdieu & Passeron, 1977).

There are major strengths in this radical framework. As a model for inquiry, it may rightly identify a dysfunctional or unintended consequence of an otherwise rational system. The inequality may not be a goal and its reproduction may be accidental. A social construction of reality reveals a type of "pathology of consciousness" that must be overcome (Hassard, 1991, p. 277). Moreover, wherever one employs a rational and efficient action to achieve organizational ends, someone or some group will necessarily suffer. For example, to achieve learning ends, class discipline may be required. Organizations may not be inherently neutral as researchers have believed: The radical thinkers may be correct in highlighting the gross ideological elements here (Capper, 1993; Evers & Lakomski, 1991; Morgan, 1986).

As a normative mechanism for achieving social change, the radical framework may well be an excellent approach. Critical thinkers speak for the exploited groups. Radicals also may counter the other, more conventional frameworks, which have their own vested interests. Radicals seem to explain quite well why teacher strikes, parent-school board conflicts, and other divisions occur in our society.

Morgan (1986) pointed out that radicals may yet provide a new and aggressive type of social consciousness that forces those in power to look at the inhuman outcomes of their practices.

The radical framework seems paranoid at times (Morgan, 1986). Lurking behind every decision and every policy is the willful intent to disenfranchise some group or other. Radical theorists seem overly committed to an assumed conspiracy theory with respect to educational organizations. Accidental and unintended consequences are seen as planned. Capper (1993) accurately summarizes the failings of radical framing: Radicals are deeply rooted in rationality and structure (Liston, 1988); are more focused on class than other categories (such as gender, race, etc.); privilege those possessing articulate speech and position (following Habermas, 1993), such that children and women are rarely heard from or listened to (Ellsworth, 1989); and push for consensus that may mask conflicting views and interests. In addition, domination theory tends to mobilize opposition to a problem but in so doing often achieves only marginal change. We may wonder if school leaders do not become overly sensitive to critique and thus become paralyzed. Radicals may actually petrify problems, generate sides in issues, and slow the effective resolution of difficulties (Morgan, 1986). Domination thinking may blind us to organizations that are not domination oriented. Researchers are thus less able to distinguish exploitative from nonexploitative organizations. Finally, domination theory is ideological, and although other frameworks may exhibit ideological features, these thinkers seem to take this to the extreme.

Some feminists (Ellsworth, 1989) strongly reject critical theory and critical administration for failing to allow for gender discourse. Power continues to reside in White males, and women and minorities have heretofore only responded to the power of that voice. These feminists contend that only by evading the rational dialogue with men may women gain control over their own discourse-practice. It is possible to fuse some of the concerns of the feminists and critical theorists, however. Capper (1993) sees both sectors cautious in their embrace of poststructuralist-postmodernist agenda: Both see the retention of theory as essential to the continuous critique of the disabling power relations in organizations.

Humanist Framework

Standard frameworks thinking finds a fourth cluster of theoretical mind-sets (Clark, Astuto, Foster, Gaynor, & Hart, 1994). Within this framework are lumped sociological subjectivists committed to radical change, some feminists, and critical theorists not captured by the radical camp. It has been argued that postmodernism seems to fit the humanist framework because it holds to a constructed reality, wishes to wrest power from the dominant group, and seeks to counter orthodox themes (Clark et al., 1994).

The humanist frame seems to operate as a catch-all category. Widely different groups of researchers are placed within it. This frame poses a unique problem for frameworks thinking because it fails to exclude members who have commitments to parts of the other frames.

The Critique of Frameworks Thinking

Critics have found advantages and disadvantages with the so-called frameworks approach to viewing organizations. The term *framework* is a metaphor and assumes that the language of construction or museum work is apropos to school life. Frameworks imply rigid braces and connectors, points of intersection, all linear and coordinated. Instead of planes of existence from geometry or facets of gemology, we are led to believe that schools as organizations manifest longitudinal parts and coordinates of intersection that lend balance to analysis and study. But the metaphors of the museum are richer, replacing *framing* with *design, butt joints* with *coloring*. Instead of the rough-hewn post-and-beam construction language, we may move to an artistic rendering that emphasizes the brightness, intensity, and motion found in schools as sites of artistic life.

Each of these four frameworks employs polarized concepts, such as "effective versus ineffective," "motivated versus unmotivated," "mature versus immature," and "empowered versus unempowered," and then goes on to describe school organizations as sharply different based on such variables being evident. Data are collected and generalizations set forth but based on the lens deemed appropriate to the researcher. The assumption that antagonisms between polar concepts are real and warrant the search for specifications of such opposites is never questioned.

We need a meaningful way of speaking about organizations that does not fall heir to the difficulties of these four frameworks and that provides a method by which the frameworks notion may be carefully reconstructed to produce the greatest understanding of school life. Can we go beyond frameworks and paradigms as we inquire into organizations such as schools? I propose that research methodology has progressed from concern with concepts and terms (operational definitions), theories, conceptual schemes, frameworks, and paradigms to a more global way of life. At each level of abstraction, researchers encountered philosophical and theoretical problems with language and practice. These debates were interminable. Hence, current research is ready to abandon the controversial issue of framework and paradigm and to speak of inquiry as conducted within a whole orientation to living.

The key difficulties with frameworks thinking that prompt this move to higher ground are many. Frameworks or paradigms research has attached to it the simple recommendation that there must be plural ways to look at things. To the extent that we are encouraged to adopt differing points of view regarding matters, multiple frameworks are an advance over uniform and singular visions of states of affairs. However, the four frameworks conception of the world of educational organizations is flawed for several reasons.

Evers and Lakomski (1991) have pointed out that paradigms include substantive theories as well as the criteria for evaluating these theories. These paradigms in effect contain different ways of dealing with knowledge. Social and educational researchers have elevated this belief into an embrace of multiple paradigms. It is assumed that research findings within these respective frames are relatively true for adherents to the frame and relatively false for nonadherents. A *myth of radical relativism* is embraced that at once propagates the plural worlds framed and the research concepts and tools relative to these worlds as viable and relatively successful, while leaving open the question of how to judge between one framework and plural frameworks.

A second faulty assumption underwriting frameworks thinking is attached to the serial nature of research frames. Earlier frames are historical in nature and are replaced as newer and different theory nets emerge. A device that triggers change must be introduced, and this is a function of the *overall theory of framework change*. This device may be evolution, revolution, devolution, progress, faddism, and so on. The important point is that researchers shift from one frame to the next for some reasons not embedded in the particular frame itself.

A third fallacy attached to the successive frameworks characterization of researcher orientation toward educational organizations is the *myth of the metanarrative*. Frameworks theory, for its success, requires that we accept an overarching set of metalevel assumptions regarding the mechanisms by which framing operates. For example, the metanarrative of frameworking in educational administration presumes the virtue of systematic depiction, coherent and cohesive rendition, and shared understanding. The precise steps utilized in working up research descriptions are warranted by the assumed logical and discrete nature of these procedures, completeness of outcomes, and so forth. The metanarrative is a tale that is believed but rarely told.

Last, a species of the metanarrative objection is found in complaints that the frameworks conception is *ideological* in cases in which particular advocates of a frame refuse to entertain other frameworks as viable renditions.

Certainly one of the most knotty problems for frame theorists to account for is the emergence and strength of new frames. Within frame theory, a particular framework has no place for disconfirming data. The inputs from research observations are sorted into accepted categories, or they are not perceived at all. Shifts from one framework to another are the result of inputting activities but only if the frames are somehow connected so that an item of information or observation may be transferred as an addition or replacement (Diesing, 1991).

Researchers should not assume that they may posit a set of research frameworks that they may enter or leave at will. It cannot be said that educational organizational researchers can claim their core assumptions simply by willing them to change. Granted that social scientists are trained to understand multiple points of view—thus being able to critique intellectual work—they simply are not able to shift their core assumptions relative to the nature of the universe (chaos vs. cosmos), the nature of human nature, and what counts as knowledge and what does not (Parker & McHugh, 1991). The gross separation of research into quantitative and qualitative types is an example of this difficulty in which researchers seem less flexible in moving from one to the other.

Needed is an understanding of the soft side of research paradigms, with their lack of well-fortified boundaries on the one hand and the rather rigid and insular nature of the work that goes on within relative paradigms and frameworks. This tough-minded approach to research paradigms overlooks communication across frames so that a theorist in one frame may accept what was heretofore disconfirming data. According to Bernstein (1983), this factor of communicability is inimical to all theorizing: Frameworks and paradigms find resident theorists knowing rival paradigms all too well. They just do not agree with the other frameworks perspective on the essential researchable problems and the appropriate means for their resolution.

Perhaps the most significant criticism of the frameworks approach to the study of educational administration is that the frameworks approach itself is a framework. It assumes the multiple perspectives yet demonstrates a single perspective on the problem of educational administration research. Pluralist in specification and absolutist in origin, the frames possess an inherent dilemma. If it is true that there are multiple frames, then a notion of multiple discrete frames is one such frame. However, if it is just another option, it is possible for another frame to emerge that discredits it. Such a possibility appears in a nonfoundational vision of framing that disallows the naive objectivism supporting multiple frameworks thinking.

Parker and McHugh (1991), in their critique of John Hassard's (1991) article "Multiple Paradigms and Organizational Analysis: A Case Study," point out that Hassard's effort to conduct research within four distinct frameworks following Burrell and Morgan (1979) is actually an effort within a fifth framework. These writers correctly see that Hassard's relativization of research practice is not multi-paradigmatic but rather a research effort informed by metatheoretical beliefs. Coherent and neat, Hassard seems to assume that the

Burrell and Morgan frames are distinct "entities" (Parker & McHugh, 1991, p. 454).

Each of these so-called frameworks suffers from inadequacies. A new orientation is needed—a new way of thinking about schools that does not fall heir to the problems encountered by these four frameworks and that goes beyond frameworks thinking.

Despite the richness attributed to frameworks and the flexibility to see them in differing contexts and against differing individuals, the frameworks approach to organizations is still more modern than postmodern and more structural than poststructural. As Foster (1986) correctly pointed out, the idea of competing frameworks or lenses through which to examine organizations does not help in understanding which human experiences may be within such life worlds as schools. We are left to wonder what difference such architectures of thought make in the day-to-day work of school administrators, teachers, and students. Is there not a better way to think about the problem of school arrangements?

Poststructuralism, Pragmatism, and Restructuring of Schools

Currently the call of reformers is one of restructuring the schools of our nation. Beneath most plans for restructure are found fundamental assumptions regarding the nature of the school and the capacity of theory to enable its reconfiguration. The four frameworks previously discussed are to a greater or lesser extent structuralist attempts to observe, report on, and manipulate a type of virtual reality of educational function. Suffering from an antiseptic and formalistic mind-set, restructurers assume that by moving certain pieces of the system and the authority and decision-making aspects of these parts, a better school organization will result.

Structuralism

Structuralism as a research metanarrative perceives organizations (such as schools) to be orderly systems capable of rational description and understanding. The structuralist has lent credence to a cult of professional expertise and specialization over lay investigation and participation. Linear means-end thinking rather than creative speculation dominates. The individual child or teacher is decentered and seen as essentially powerless, whereas the organizational structure is of primary controlling importance.

Because structuralism looks to the repetitive and similar, the nonrepetitive and dissimilar phenomena are unseen. Structuralism has an inherent bias against change. The frameworks approach stresses the reasonable and discursive over the irrational and voiceless. As Lyotard (1984) pointed out, legitimate practices in organizations gain their value from "performativity," or the technical and systemic features of input and output. School leaders are told to enhance their individual and school effectiveness by realigning the power sources for maximal school test performance. The additional result is that the language of effectivity empowers those enforcing the rules of the language game of structuralism.

Poststructuralism

Poststructuralists reject the assumptions of the structuralists regarding organizations. This new way of thinking about organizations has emerged in the research literature and offers great promise in unraveling the problems students, teachers, administrators, and parents face in navigating the 12 years of schooling (Fazzaro, Walter, & McKerrow, 1994).

In the past it has been possible for educational administration researchers to operate as if there were substantial metalevel criteria that enabled the enterprise. The so-called scientific approach to educational administration phenomena accepted the notion that schools and educational personnel could be studied like physical events in the laboratory. There was one scientific method, and it was appropriate for the examination of educational states of affairs, just as physicists applied this method to physical science phenomena. Positivism, logical empiricism, and other terms were applied to variations of this metanarrative, but this fundamental assumption underwrote research for decades (and in some spheres continues to the present day).

Critical Pragmatism

Pragmatism has a strong affinity for much of poststructuralism. It does not fit the frameworks model. As Clark et al. (1994) have noted, pragmatism rejects the scientific framework because it is wrong to assume school organizations display an underlying structure that may be discovered by scientific methods. Pragmatism parts company with the interpretivists because they overemphasize the subjectivity of the organizational inquirer and posit a world that is fundamentally unstable and sometimes chaotic. Pragmatists are not accepting of the humanist framework because rational communication and consensus regarding perceived underlying forms of domination are not singular and unique ways of dealing with social conflict.

Pragmatists call for "intellectual moves" that involve concern for voice and participation through dialogue and debate, critical and aesthetic intelligence, and an emphasis on the efforts to reconstruct community. The focus is on the changing nature of cultural conditions and the poststructural efforts to reconceptualize social living (Rorty, 1991). Research in educational organizations may be engaged in best through the use of these pragmatic procedures. These techniques or skills would not be tethered to a metanarrative framework, nor would they be statements of so-called fact. I propose to investigate schools by using processes, particularly those attached to moral understanding and aesthetic realms of practice, that would move educational inquirers toward an understanding of education without the baggage of frameworks and the difficulties they possess.

The solution adopted here is one of *critical pragmatism.* However, the idea of critical pragmatism stresses some historical aspects of pragmatism over others. The pages that follow explain a pragmatic stance that emphasizes discussion, artistic-moral intelligence, and community as reformist values. Critical pragmatism is a philosophic view deriving from key social pragmatist thinkers such as John Dewey, Arthur Bentley, and others but with new poststructural elements that make it appropriate for the postliberal democratic culture of the 21st century.

The term *critical pragmatism* was first used by Abraham Kaplan in *American Ethics and Public Policy* (1958) and has become popularized recently by Cleo Cherryholmes in his book *Power and Criticism* (1988). Cherryholmes identified four critical pragmatic strategies: (a) reading, (b) interpretation, (c) criticism, and (d) communication. The thrust of critical pragmatism in this text entails some of their arguments, but others are developed in addition. Critical pragmatism, like postmodernism-poststructuralism, blanches at the self-description of "method." There is no simple patterned sequence of steps for problem solving such as the scientific method. Nor is pragmatism a framework. Critical pragmatism is a process of reflection that takes seriously certain considerations of mind and value, deploying these in critical thought.

The role of this critical pragmatism is to refocus attention on the concrete problems in social organizations such as schools, viewing these problems as matters to be carefully analyzed and discussed. By deploying this brand of critique on metaphors such as "framework" to provide understandings of what is at stake and what may be required of our modes of inquiry, we may release research from its dogmatic past. The pragmatist as a critic must encourage dialogue about and across frames, aiding investigators as well as participants in schools to see the fundamental assumptions and values that regulate our inquiries. The task is not to force consensus but rather to keep the dialogue going and to promote the edification necessary to at once enhance the status and development of individual members of communities and enlarge the possibilities of democratic culture itself (Rorty, 1989).

This agenda for critical pragmatism is particularly appealing for school reform given the postmodern nature of contemporary American culture and the rising number of interest groups on the horizon. This philosophy is a type of policy analysis posture that allows for the reasoned inquiry into the many claims on the purposes of the public school. Within this approach is a set of norms that guides us in the deployment of critical judgment relative to the competing claims on our institutions. An archeology is offered that elevates our thought and practice relative to schooling and democratic life.

It is significant that pragmatism has certain preferences when it comes to inquiry modes, culture, and social organization. Although there certainly are differences in particular pragmatists' views of religion, knowledge, and so forth, it is possible to speak of a pragmatic view that entails many historical pieces of pragmatic theory. In addition, pragmatism as I have outlined it in the following pages shows a strong affinity for poststructuralism-postmodernism and postliberal political theory.

Core Process Values of Critical Pragmatism

Schools are seen as social institutions, as cultures, as climates, and as political arenas. Social scientists speak of social rules, roles, and relationships; myths, rituals, and folklore; psychoses and neuroses; and oppression and empowerment of political actors. Often the vocabularies and theories differ from scholarly discipline to scholarly discipline. What is represented and how it is spoken of are matters of debate and argument (Bentley, 1954).

Yet in the American instance, public schools today are said to manifest such differences and so many irregularities that it is nearly impossible to generalize about them, to stand back far enough to see the larger world of schooling. Diverse in population and pluralistic in arrangement, schools are treated as miniature societies, toy-cultures, play-governments, and freeze-dried institutions. At the base level of day-to-day existence, similarities and differences provide the best characterizing features of educational units facing reorganization. However, we have so neglected the day-to-day experiences of the people within schools and surrounding communities that it is difficult to see the stories, creative features, and communal character of these schools.

In the place of sociological, anthropological, political, and psychological efforts to engage in vocabulary reification by creating metaphors and then employing a reductionism by assigning collected data and descriptions to these abstract categories, let us turn to a philosophic motif. The key enabling values that inform our pragmatic view of American society and culture, although sensitive to these social sciences, should be divorced from the scientific, structured, formalistic, and rarefied intellectualism that dominates subfields such as educational administration research.

Critical pragmatism proposes looking at frameworks, patterns, and other metaphors as intellectual devices to smooth research efforts and provide short takes on human life and institutions.

Sociology, anthropology, political science, and psychology all lend their theories and vocabularies to the enterprise of making sense of this world. However, needed is a wiser view that critiques such inadequate research efforts as well as realigns our inquiry in terms of the values so sorely lacking in public life today. The core values in this pragmatic philosophy are clustered around three themes.

Theme One: Communication

Freire (1973) impressed on us first the power of silence and the invidious results of lack of consciousness of our condition. The key to any viable theory of school reform is found in a new understanding of the articulation of individuals and their interests. Speech allows the individual person to reveal herself or himself as unique. Labor and work fail to disclose human identity. Conversation forms the essence of reconstructive thought (Arendt, 1958).

To apply debate to the arena of school reform, it is essential to lay down the groundwork assumptions that inform this position. Arendt elevates debate from mere verbal controversy to argumentative discourse-action. Debating is a type of acting. Conversely, acting is intricately related to speaking. Pragmatists stress the value of speech and action as means for persons to reveal themselves and affirm their identity (d'Entreves, 1989). Pragmatists prefer to see all speech as connected with concrete or hypothetical actions.

Both pragmatism and postmodernism-poststructuralism accept alternative modes of expression to that of a single reasoned scientific discourse. Human experience is often metaphorically spoken of as a "text." Characters and events come to be inscribed or written on the space of schools. The task of thought is to recover these texts and critique them.

Narrative tales communicate a culture. Fenwick English (1994) used biographies of great leaders to reveal characteristics of leadership appropriate for school administrators. The use of metaphor and myth to explain leadership in education is an exciting means for enlarging our understanding of these institutions. Julia Kristeva (1986) has examined modes of folkloristic expression that appear irrational but when viewed in more primitive ways appear as sublimely insightful. Baudrillard (1993) provided new ways to speak of our postmodern condition as simulations of liberation.

Pragmatists use metaphors cautiously, conducting tests of adequacy based on concrete consequences in experience. Thus the metaphors of school as laboratory or battleground, for example, are fruitful only insofar as the results in practice yield growth in the richness of experienced educational value. Metaphors for school organization have taken on lives of their own, however. We have failed to hold them up to the light of critical pragmatic inquiry. Now we must do so because newer and richer metaphors are needed that serve the interests of a postmodern culture and its inhabitants.

Theme Two: Moral Artistry-Intelligence

Aesthetic design. Action in the form of artistic work allows for more scope for individuality to come into play; however, it reveals our similarity to others as well. In artistic work (*technē*) or productive achievement (*poiēsis*) the worker is still guided by others in the form of models and in the fact that the final result is to outlast the artist. The artistic performance does not reveal much about the maker, so for Arendt (1958) aesthetic work is not much richer than labor. Work of an artistic nature does not need a "who" attached to it, either.

Intelligent inquiry is given strength and point through an artistic disposition. Required is a form of discourse about schools as social spaces in which we may rehearse, or test out, the moral-ethical drama of action. Artistic and moral-ethical values are crucial. Rather than view schooling in a structured manner, let us look at a better entry point as one of an enlightened composition for schools to be found in aesthetics. Fesmire (1994) has argued cogently for the need of aesthetics as dramatic rehearsal for the restoration of societal equilibrium. The aesthetic we find in Dewey is one of artful deliberation. Although the pressures of the situation and our psychological disposition toward the problematization of experience exist, art is the awareness of the openness of experience to different forms. Through moral deliberation we come to deal with competing desires regarding what shall be primary. In this way an experience becomes a standard for practice. And, for Dewey, *the* ideal of social living was democracy. Hence we are moral just insofar as we are able to bring this ideal into being.

Intelligence. Drawing on pragmatic intelligence, in light of the work of Raup, Axtelle, Benne, and Smith (1943/1950) and Bode (1938), the collective problems of our day may be identified and critical inquiry may begin. Dewey, like Giroux today, proposed that communities and publics be given the salient matters of fact-value and encouraged to debate alternative routes to resolution (Dewey, 1927/ 1955; Dewey, 1935; Giroux, 1988d).

Pragmatism and poststructuralism reject the notion that there is one single rationality by which all propositions are to be tested. Propositional knowledge is subject to criticism, and beyond this the criticism itself may be criticized. It is here that poststructuralism and pragmatism share another feature: Both undertake the criticism of criticisms. When we attempt to gain an understanding of educational organizations, following the above maxim, it is important to see the description and explanation of schools as open to critique.

If poststructuralists and critical pragmatists are skeptical of universal criteria for establishing truth, they also reject any single brand of rationality. Poststructuralists celebrate the irrational and engage in efforts not to construct architectonic organizational edifices but to deconstruct and thus reconstruct organizations (Rosenau, 1992). Finally, critical pragmatists in particular wish to conceive of research not as final and finished but as tentative and open.

Antifoundationalism. There can be no sanctified and secure perch from which to observe the passing show. This lack of any single foundation, or metanarrative, is pervasive in the theories of postmodernists and pragmatists alike. Bernstein (1983) maintained that pragmatists reject the notion of a foundational view or Archimedean point from which theories and philosophies may be judged acceptable or unacceptable. In short, there is no permanent, value-neutral matrix of instant rationality against which to test school life.

However, it is equally important to see that there is no special place in which the critic may stand to judge the value of his or her tools except within the language game itself. Discourses are at once relativized, but by saying this, we are not seeking to place the characterizing on another, higher foundational plane. As Rorty (1979) has pointed out, this has been the problem for philosophy since the Enlightenment and has yielded nothing in its exercise.

But if there are no foundational givens on which the school enterprise rests, where do we stand? Bernstein (1983), Rorty (1979), and, much earlier, Dewey (1929), Wittgenstein (1953), and Heidegger (1927/1962) all supported the retreat from a foundational perspective. They rejected the idea that there is some basic set of criteria by which to judge the acceptability of truth claims in the social sciences. Following this line of reasoning, educational organizational research is mistaken in its efforts to ground its inquiry in any set of foundational framework assumptions regarding what it references.

When poststructuralists reject the idea that objects and events are impossible to characterize using a theory-neutral language, they have in mind the notion that experiences and characters are relative to different discourses. This relativity of description-explanation is not reduced to any metanarrative or superlanguage. In some senses, the regular and ordered patterns of things are as much the result of our language as they are of the innate structure of the universe. Language and truth do not match the real world. The correspondence theory of truth is illicit, as Dewey had early argued. In this nonfoundational theory of language and representation, the postmodernist and pragmatist are partners.

Today, there certainly are multiple interpretations of the world of schools. Part of the disagreement over what must be done to reform schools grows from a single corresponding version to the truth of school phenomena. Add to this the fact of too much data and too little cogent theory to use in making understandable conjectures as to what is true or false, and you have some explanation of our quandary.

Critical judgment. The type of intelligence needed for examining schools is both critical and practical. Reflective thinking is a type of mentality that not only recognizes facts and values but also sees problems calling for specifying what should be done. Rather than professional rhetoric, we need ordinary words and ideas in our analysis of schools and restructuring.

Although for some researchers a new, frameless approach elicits horror, for others it seems to provide a procedural stance that is fresh in its conception. Bernstein (1992) argued that this nonfoundational view allows for continuous fruitfulness critique—a deep criticism that fails to produce reconciliation or consensus but is nonetheless vital to the life of a culture. For Rorty (1979), it is enough that the conversation continues: The epistemological mission is no longer central. Because truth has been defined relative to differing and competing frameworks, the central task is not to seek truth but to explore literature and other forms of expression. It is also possible while adopting a nonfoundationalist perspective to slip back into a realist conception of the world and do battle at the level of inter-theory evaluation and test (Evers & Lakomski, 1991). Thus, nonfoundationalisms differ.

Poststructuralists studying school restructuring necessarily introduce critique into their research. The entire notion of restructure assumes that there is a structure and that it can be observed and manipulated. Poststructuralists find no such thing. School restructuring as a movement tends to fuse the optative mood, a disposition to judge between true or false reports of what the structure anticipates; the imperative mood is seen as mere adjustment of the categories and relationships of the structure as proposed (Childs, 1956).

Certainly one way out of the hornet's nest of "nature of research" questions is to switch from truth seeking to meaning seeking (some would even introduce the goal of wisdom seeking). And in this we may embrace a critical pragmatic and poststructural process approach to the current school restructuring phenomenon. For the discourse-practice of organizational change to be viable, it is necessary to enter into modes of thought that embrace the larger posture we as humans take toward our experience. We could, given this move, become concerned with the search for *craft* in administrative behavior, teaching acts, learning postures, and so forth. Here the artful design, symbolic expression, and harmonious performance serve as expressions that are sorely lacking in administration discourse (Maxcy, 1991). It is possible following Barber and McGrath (1982) to see talk of *vision* as flattened, discordant—ruled by a rational-technical world view that sees aesthetics as engineered efficiency—and to speak of artistry (performative or other) crafting plans of the new school order that is both critical and emancipatory.

Instead of the metaphor of framework, we should adopt the characterization of schools as moral-ethical compositions. Such a metaphor allows the freeing up of aesthetic, moral, and ethical language for the purpose of evaluating schooling and school arrangements. The school may be spoken of as a type of illuminated manuscript on which are drawn richly colored inscriptions of treasured impressions.

Composition of the good school. We should attempt to locate the good social entity through aesthetics. Aesthetics opens up the objects of our attention to growth, action, and method. Morality is artistic when we engage in dramatic rehearsals. Art is experience when it is clarified and intensified. Composition is essential. We may speak, as Bateson (1989) has, of composing a life. For Dewey, it was the organizational features of moral experience—what form it takes—that makes it moral, or scientific, and so on (Fesmire, 1994). Of course we could in an experimentalist frame of mind build our moral philosophy on a naturalist posture as John Childs (1950/1967) did, but my preference is to go at it from the aesthetic instead, if for no other reason than naturalism and evolutionism seem to be less descriptive of the problematics of the postmodern era we face.

We should not overlook the fact that humans require freedom to be creative. When we live in overly controlled social spaces, most of our experiences are neither meaningful nor fulfilling (Dewey, 1934). Form is the active and temporal continuity of interaction that the artistic work brings about so that *an* experience can be transformed into a consummatory event (Alexander, 1987).

Finally, our core moves ought to relate the realm of human values to the enterprise of school reform. Heretofore the efforts of school restructurers, in the United States in particular, have neglected moral, ethical, artistic, and other values by merely assuming them. This text will offer a means through which our most cherished values may be linked to concrete educational choices to make them more instrumental to the individual and collective good.

Experience. Although some critical pragmatists and poststructuralists offer the metaphor of *text* as equivalent to school, of interest here is seeing schooling as sets of experiences. Not every experience will do, as Dewey (1934) wrote in *Art as Experience:* We must shoot for the "consummatory experience" (p. 55). The conclusion is not the end but rather an outcome that organizes and unifies the experience. This unification is a distinct, intense, and integrative quality. We should be after a type of intense experience that guides us. Unifying and organizing various parts of the experience as a whole help us work toward the overall end we seek. Such an experience is formed gradually and is laden with a sense of immanent possibility and progressive realization (Alexander, 1987). In this way, the consummatory experience becomes one and the same with the moral ideal.

To a large extent, talk of frameworks in educational administration research is an exercise in simulating. Frameworks are linguistic shorthand devices that seek not to map the terrain of institutional experience but to highlight key intersections of such experience. These frames seek to differentiate elements in experience and to demonstrate repetitions and regularities of such elements. The form of the framework is a stable structure; the datum of experience is assumed to be equally structured. Often it is turned on suspected hegemonies and inequalities; rarely has critique functioned in a fully culturally reconstructive way. On this subject Jean Baudrillard, the French philosopher and media critic, is informative (see Poster, 1988). Baudrillard engages in a critique that is neither political-ideological nor framework oriented. For Baudrillard, the reality of the postmodern world is hidden behind simulations. Simulation follows on simile, with the simulation masquerading as the actual, but is not identical with it.

The implications of this type of analysis are informative: Schools as organizations may posture as a variety of structured enterprises. The restructuring will thus entail a reform of a reflection of other structures. We see this in reforms that seek to restructure the schools along purely efficient lines, with smoother paper flows and easier record keeping. The essential fit of a business or corporate model to schools is suspicious in the first place, but reforms that seek to make schools qua businesses more effective may well perpetuate the simulacrum.

Process and meliorism. Pragmatism entails a belief in process and the fruitfulness of intervening to make things better (*meliorism*). Critique requires a processual approach to organizational form, as Arthur Bentley pointed out in his early text in political science, *The Process of Government* (1908/1967). This book revolutionized the way in which government courses were taught. In the place of formal categories such as "executive branch" and trivial lockstep characterizations such as "how a bill becomes a law," Bentley postulated governing as a set of behaviors and processes. His *Behavior Knowledge Fact* (1935) undercut the positivism of science and social science by raising the question: What is a social fact? In answer to this query, Bentley proposed a theory of observation and communication that was revolutionary for its time. Last, *Knowing and the Known* (Dewey & Bentley, 1949) attacked the terminology of epistemology, calling for more accurate words to name the transactions of human social units.

Theme Three: Community

Dewey (1927/1946) spoke of a triad of ideas: communication, common, and community. He rightly believed that by sharing our common ideas and values in conversation we could create community.

School reform is best pursued within an open public space—a community—in which free debate and argumentation are encouraged. The resultant actions of school reordering should therefore be a product of the conjoint communication-action of the persons most affected by the rearrangements. Public forums of all interested parties must be held. Dialogue and discussion are to be encouraged. The resulting reconfiguration is not to be rehearsed or overly structured by elites and experts.

Needed is *democratic authority* over authoritarianism in school reform. Totalitarian authority renders the human condition controlled but inert. Democratic authority is not universally recognized within the public schools of the United States. Certainly one device to promote such democratization is a freeing of students, teachers, administrators, and parents within schools, an artistic form of liberating democracy. The powerlessness felt by many educators in the schools today is a symptom of a deep moral-ethical illness attached to the way our educational institutions are organized.

Pluralism. Human groups are collectivities of individuals bound by shared beliefs, concerns, and attitudes. Although physical characteristics of humans such as skin color and hair type may vary across racial lines, it is only as these differences become of interest to groups that they form boundaries of specialty. We must not overlook the capacity of human intelligence to seize on difference as a warrant for a variety of aims, goals, and plans. It is not a long trip from recognition of difference and formation of interest in such difference to erecting borders separating and dividing membership in the group. When such interests result in wholehearted efforts to enlarge the richness of life, we have a genuine normative cultural pluralism; however, when such interests are used to privilege a group and rigidify its relations with outsiders, we have dysfunction.

Groups within a cultural pluralism must have occasions to come into contact and to grow relative to such encounters. Rather than conflict and disagreement, the focus needs to be on the interests that bring groups together to share. Dewey (1916b) long ago talked of the "hyphenated American," someone who was at once Jewish-Irish-Polish-Swedish and so forth (pp. 183-189). He emphasized that it was those matters that joined us that made us what we were, not the things that separated us. The more interests we come to have in common, regardless of our physical characteristics, the more important our democracy would become.

How shall we make institutions sensitive to differences that are legitimate yet resistant to differences that are illicit and dangerous? This is possible only through the importation of moral responsibility into the process of institutional structuring. Smiley (1992) has argued that responsibility interfaces with social problems in two ways: We wonder what role responsibility plays in our efforts to resolve such problems, and we wonder how responsibility affects our identification of such problems in the first place. Translated into our problem of diversity, placing blame for certain actions is not a matter of discovering objective *causes* for such harm but rather a matter of importing into our judgments of blame certain social and cultural attitudes whose interests count in our society. Moreover, when we attempt to set *blame* in psychological terms, we also import cultural assumptions about when individual persons can be expected to control their own behavior.

The boundaries that separate diverse peoples in American society today are built on interests. It is not so much the physical appearances or the cultural practices that distinguish us as it is the meanings such differences take on through interest. We must work to locate the mutually satisfying interests across groups and to capitalize on these. Division is not important in its own right: Only differences that make life meaningful and rich are to be supported by a reconfigured school. Just as there are distinctions to be made in curriculum, there are differences to be made and argued for in social life. The important point is to see such interests as emerging in dialogue and debate.

The moral becomes a matter of responsibility as we self-reflect on these sources of preconditioning for setting causes and blameworthiness. Morality requires the other; it requires a community.

Ways of life. Plural forms of collective living are evident in postmodern culture. When we examine theories of human organizations, we must be alert to the relativism that is pervasive in such theorizing. Chopping the study of the universe of schooling into neat frameworks, paradigms, and conceptual schemes poses particular problems for our understanding and control of such social spaces.

The critical and dialectical features of frameworks theories are lodged primarily in the older modernist rational and scientific mode. The manner of speaking is trapped in the doublespeak of "value neutrality," "hard facts," and "real statistics." Left unanalyzed is the status of organizational depiction itself.

Critical pragmatism provides understanding of the scaffolded explanatory devices used to underwrite school research. Philosophers of science began by attending to the words and concepts as well as the constructs used in administration discourse, challenging elliptical and impoverished meanings. The next level at which philosophy sought to enter the world of administration was at the level of theory. Largely as the result of Kuhn's (1962/1970) work, philosophers were able to critique the way a particular theory was affirmed or denied. Next, because of the work of Lakatos (1970), scholars drew a bead on theory networks, or research programs. Here the logical and argumentative tools of critical philosophy were played out. Now the current playing field that philosophy has selected to address is that of ways of life. It is no longer possible to engage in vocation without consideration of the larger pattern of beliefs and practices that regulate that work. Here philosophy seems highly appropriate because philosophies are associated patterns of meaning utilized to guide practical decisions in life. It is conceivable that, by embracing a pragmatic philosophic perspective, we may find an approach to research. In current controversies there is a move away from concern about research craft (e.g., value-free data analysis) toward more global attitudes toward the researchers' beliefs about human nature, the nature of the world, and so on. In part this seems logical, given the penchant to speak of social issues and allied deprivations and inaccessibilities to the goods of social life.

In a rich pluralistic culture such as is found in the United States, communication across ethnic, racial, and gender groups may provoke a wide variety of psychological attitudes. The important point is that experience is hardly static and recursive, although criteria for understanding need not stagnate in 18th-century principles of regulated rational discourse. Efforts of members to speak across boundaries are not only natural but also to be encouraged. We ought not to push silent voices into a permanent self-imposed culture of silence. Bernstein (1983) encouraged us to engage in debate under the flag of practical rationality. Local forms of interest-based community life become linked up despite our efforts to close down communication. A search for mutual understanding is endemic to the human species. If Arendt is correct, we will find action emerging out of speech. Action for social reform of schools is necessarily embedded in dialogue. Conversation may be used to overcome divisiveness and difference or to promote separateness—but talk we must as we address practical problems of mutual importance. As West (1993) noted, we must see difference operating in differing arenas— existential, intellectual, and political. Pragmatism offers a method by which pluralism may work for the emancipation of those locked in the bonds of racism. Communication requires effort and never entails absolute certainty regarding what the other party will say. This openness is a hallmark of democratic liberalism as a plan for cultural pluralism.

The New School Order

Reconstruction. I shall expropriate themes from pragmatism and poststructuralism that seem appropriate for rethinking today's school problems. The moral life of schools has taken on renewed interest and is now seen a vital part of understanding what makes education work (Jackson, Boostrom, & Hansen, 1993). MacIntyre (1981) observed that it is difficult to recapture the historical moral discourse to explain contemporary conflicts in social institutions. The problems bureaucracies encounter are due to the absence of a sense of human beings as selves. However, the reconstruction of educational communities is a crucial necessity, and pragmatism may well yield the key to unlock a vision of schools as moral-ethical spaces in which people may live and learn.

By extrapolating the aesthetic sense to school organization, it is possible to speak of school leadership being in the business of transforming experiences into consummatory events via the reconstruction of organizational form. Educational events as temporal and continuous forms of action must be reconstructed into beautiful visions of living—communicative, communal, and common.

To accomplish such a reconstruction of schooling we must become familiar with a moral and aesthetic vocabulary, learn to use such concepts in our reform discourse, and show schools how to achieve beautiful landscapes of learning. Such a vision of the new pragmatism is incomplete without social and cultural reconstruction as an ideal (Anderson, 1990; Campbell, 1992).

Educational management modeled itself on the social sciences, subjecting school organizations, administrators, and teachers to a series of research-generated frameworks, paradigms, and other simple schemes to evoke effectiveness. Educational researchers have come to embrace two nearly equally viable methodological routes—quantitative and qualitative—in their work. Recently, however, studies of the educational administration professorate and departments of educational administration are being discussed as inhabiting a type of preparadigmatic reform period awaiting clearer direction (Pohland, 1992). Something is changing in the workaday world of school organizations.

Frameworks thinking is flawed. I propose critical pragmatism as a means for adopting a perspective that does not fall heir to the difficulties of the four frameworks version of the world of schooling while generating a more open-textured, morally and aesthetically sensitive, and fruitful option for researchers inquiring into educational organizations to follow in the future.

In the end, pragmatism will be of use when it moves us to confront our experience as meliorists in new and fresh transactional terms. Morally and aesthetically driven and transformative in spirit, pragmatism as aesthetic encounter with moral ideals—such as democracy—leads to the development of improved forms of institutional life (schools) and better means of guiding us toward these ideals (leadership over and against administration). The context of the school as a moral playground in which individuals compose more artful lives seems of priority here but with full recognition that we may grow tired of our pragmatic poetry as well as our pragmatic science. In the final analysis, we are left with our pragmatic meliorism, processes of reflection, and action. *The* revolution is eternally against structuralisms and permanent platforms and frames of all types.

Where Do We Go From Here?

Beyond the critique of frameworks, it is possible to demonstrate the point of pragmatism for the critical conduct of research in another way. When we explore a new, deeper, and more sensitive vision of human existence—postmodernism—we see how critical pragmatic philosophy may redirect our efforts as inquirers. The present endeavor is not one to create a new, improved framework, to be termed critical pragmatic poststructuralism. Rather, it shall be demonstrated that many debates have taken place regarding the place of frameworks in research practice; however, the fundamental turf that is contested is one of logical exclusivity-inclusivity rather than practical meaning. The point to be made is one of the thinking that brings us to the belief in frameworks in the first place. It is the positivist and Enlightenment rationalist in us that prompts such artificial characterizations. Granted, there are regularities and continuities in organizational life that make it organized; nevertheless, the fallacies have been those of rectification and reductionism. The architectonic universe we have constructed through the medium of organizational theory is both self-serving and idealized, with the consequence that it forms a type of modernist language game with variables and vectored forces known only to players. The experiences of living human beings are reduced to elliptical semantic structures, each presumed different from the next. Beyond the language game of frames lies the universe of unredeemed institutional experience. To capture this universe, a critically pragmatic philosophy is necessary.

We must move the debate beyond the relativism of frames and methods to a concern for employing intelligence and practical judgment, free from foundations of any type. Let us allow the competing interests within a democratic culture to bring out the best approach to the problems we face in schools as forms of associated life and learning. Within this view there is no sanctity of perspective and no mental mirroring of a single and unitary organized world of the school. The nature of the organization—its chaos and its order—is seen to emerge from transactions between the knowers and the known, with knowns shifting and changing relative to human purposes and values.

As Jackson and Carter (1991) and Bernstein (1983) accurately concluded, the frameworks approach and debate regarding framework commensurability do not offset or preclude conversation across and among frames. The argumentation has sterilized and marginalized pragmatically fruitful work. Endless controversy surrounding validity, dependent versus independent variability—all in the interest of retaining the virgin status of framework and paradigm—stifles true practical inquiry and muffles pluralism in method.

The problem in educational inquiry, exemplified by the structural frameworks theory, has been one of seeking a transcendental metanarrative, a set of external rules to judge the roles and rituals of schooling. Needed is a postmodern-poststructural philosophy that is critical in its take on organizational forms and rhetoric as well as pragmatic as it seeks to test our conceptions of organized education. The following chapters will compare and contrast, characterize and judge, and weigh and evaluate the differing theories and vocabularies of educational schema and patterns to provide pathways to better ways of talking about and living within social spaces characterized by education-associated experience.

2

Chaos Versus
Order and Our Schools

An investigation of today's schools must begin with recent directions in restructuring as indicative of the most significant reform in the last several decades. For all intents and purposes, large-scale reform of education was last successfully achieved in the first half of the 20th century with the progressive education movement. Since that time, piecemeal efforts have flourished to provide advantages to those deemed disadvantaged (Cremin, 1988). Current restructuring reforms seek the reconfiguration of the organizational layout of schooling, long a protected feature of the educational establishment. Simply rearranging the pieces of the puzzle of schooling (despite the fact that these remain illusive), contemporary restructuring overlooks the philosophic bases of education.

The present condition of many American schools is popularly viewed as chaotic—with guns, drugs, and violence hitting the top of the list as evidence. Some reformers see restructuring the chaos in schools as requiring more top-down controls, national curricula, and testing. Another strategy emphasizes relocating power and decision making in the hands of teachers, parents, and community members. Still another approach speaks of charter schools and releasing education from the grip of "the public." None of these approaches can divorce itself from the historical legacy of school organization thinking that prizes line and staff, pyramids of power, and oligarchical leadership. How school restructuring may be conceptually and valuationally warranted is overlooked, and little effort is given to exposing and reconstructing the primal beliefs that underpin current reform efforts.

Chaos Theory and School Order

Chaos theory is a new "grand theory" that takes on the systematic task not only of explaining the ultimate nature of the world or universe in theoretical terms but also of deriving from that theory a revolutionary praxis. On the face of it, this cosmology appears to be a radically new foundation for education that purports to readdress the fundamental role of disequilibrium and continuity in teaching, learning, administration, and organizational structure.

Initially, chaos theory enjoyed wide popularity in mathematics and physics. Recently theoretically oriented educational administration scholars have taken up the slogan, seeking to test it case by case in school districts across the country. Although the literature reporting on chaos theory and educational organizations is sparse, the potential is there to seek an explanation for the rapid changes in school governance in recent years (Griffiths, Hart, & Blair, 1991).

A number of questions may be raised regarding this grand theory from a pragmatic view. For example, who propounded this theory? (historical question); which groups support the theory and which do not? (sociological query); what power is at work in the advocacy of this view? (political question); and what does chaos theory mean for school reform? (philosophical question).

The Beginnings

Chaos theory is a collection of research and writing efforts in such fields as mathematics, physics, medicine, and, more recently, literature and the social sciences. Advocates focus on nonlinear change, irreversible processes, and patterns of attraction. Chaos theory typically is interested in complex systems and tends to treat such systems from a holistic standpoint.

In the area of educational organizational theory, chaos thinkers such as March and Olsen (1976) see schools as organized anarchies marked by "garbage can" decision-making strategies in the face of ambiguity. Weick (1976), following Bidwell (1965), popularized the notion that school organizations are loosely coupled. Articulation between units such as teachers, administrators, or parents is thus problematic because of the weak ties linking them. Even Herbert Simon in his early writings (1947/1965) cautioned against viewing organizations as perfect machinelike systems. Administrators, he pointed out, rarely have the time or opportunity to explore fully each option in a problematic situation; hence, organizations are fraught with "satisfying" behaviors in which leaders choose the best option, realizing it is not the ideal solution to their difficulty. Rather than assuming that educational phenomena are structured and rationally determinable, these chaos thinkers challenge the assumption that order is inherent in school organizations.

In a mathematical paper in 1890, Henri Poincaré demonstrated that a new type of math and science was required to account for the dynamics of complex systems. Although physicists had relied on linear functions, there was a need for a new nonlinear approach to dynamic systems if they were to be understood. In 1931, Kurt Godel proved that formal systems could not be axiomized completely. The way was paved for researchers to develop post-Newtonian chaos approaches to the matter of complexity (Hayles, 1990).

In the field of literary criticism, something similar was happening. Here books were reconceptualized as texts whose boundaries were arbitrary rather than fixed. Instead of attempting to locate the author's meaning or the embedded singular message of a book, the new critics argued that text meaning was dependent on who did the reading and why they read it. The French deconstructionists, such as Jacques Derrida and François Lyotard, challenged the authority of the text by speaking of "traces" and other little suspected features of writings. Books as texts were webs of word sets that demonstrated chaos rather than order (Hayles, 1990).

Certain 19th-century philosophers lent their support to chaos theory. Friedrich Nietzsche in particular broke with the orderly systems approach employed by philosophy. His books *The Birth of Tragedy and the Genealogy of Morals* (1956) and *Thus Spake Zarathustra* (1967) challenged rationalistic explanation, and *Beyond Good and Evil* (1949) broke traditional bounds by postulating a "transvaluation of value." Nietzsche was quick to point out that Western civilization had come to the point of thinking in dialectical terms. This habit of mind was traceable to the ancient Greeks but had reached a high point in the work of Hegel. Nietzsche's later philosophy focuses on the critique of the dialectics. He argued that the assumption that between the opposites of the dialectic was to be found some logical truth was seriously amiss. Because for Nietzsche logic was merely a game growing out of the human love for order rather than the search for truth, this synthesis was of doubtful status (Lenson, 1987).

Today theorists in every field from agriculture to zoology see chaos theory as informative in explaining matters in new ways. Within education, a group of theorists (Doll, 1993; March & Olsen, 1976; Oliver & Gershman, 1989; Weick, 1976) have proposed that anarchy and disorder characterize educational states of affairs as well. Teaching, administration, and student learning are examples of chaos in action. Rather than tending toward order, school systems are moving toward disorder and irregularity. Strategies are suggested, particularly in the area of curriculum redesign, that will capitalize on this type of change (Doll, 1993). In the area of educational administration, chaos theory is taken alternatively as the answer to making a new science of leadership (Sungaila, 1990) or as just another revival of the educational administration as a science argument (Green & Bigum, 1993).

Characteristics of Chaos Theory

Chaos theory first appeared in the writings of physicists and their popularizers. Gleick (1987) revealed that chaos theory presupposes that things must be looked at as systems. At the heart of chaos theory is the assumption that the parts are understandable only in terms of the whole. Moreover, the whole is more than the simple sum of the parts. Something more is involved in the system than the analyzable features of that system. This holistic view is not new. Holism has been a significant theory for much of our philosophic history.

Another characteristic of chaos theory is the belief that large systems are complex rather than simple. If we say the system is chaotic, part of what we mean is that the system is moving toward greater confusion because of the density of features displayed.

Chaos theory proposes that elements of a system and the system itself are in flux. The nature of this change over time is nonlinear. Whatever is examined in a system will be found to manifest breaks and discontinuities rather than smoothly connected transitions. The system, on inspection, reveals chaos (the system is in disarray or disorder of a serious type).

Change is symptomatic of complex systems. The gaps and fissures in the system tend toward more order (physical scientists believe this) or more disorder (literary critics hold this view). This emphasis on change places chaos theory in the group of philosophic views characterized as process theory and thus seems to have some affinity to scientific versions of pragmatism, such as that of Charles S. Peirce (1934/1963b). However, although chaos theory postulates a chaos-order pulsating system, the scientific pragmatism of Peirce saw the universe moving toward order. However, both the chaos theorists and Peirceans argue that the cosmos is gradually moving humans away from the power of choice.

Chaos theory finds that all complex systems manifest *asymmetry*. The order detected in chaotic systems is transitional and a function of the search for *equilibrium*. Jean Piaget's developmental view of the child is offered as an example of disequilibrium moving to a higher stage through a search for equilibration, and he thus is offered up as a chaos theorist. It is further proposed that systems that allow for feedback into the system manifest a *recursive symmetry* between levels and scales. This feedback function reveals order out of chaos. Computer-generated *fractals* are an example of recursion in action. The theoretical biologist Robert M. May stated that the equation $y = 4hx(1 - x)$ should be studied by having students iterate it on a calculator. Students of math thus would learn intuitively about nonlinear systems (Hofstadter, 1985, p. 387). These mathematical feedback loops reveal another feature of chaotic systems: *strange attractors.* Any chaotic system tends to generate unique patterning, but the essential catalyst for these new patterns is nonordinary. A chaotic system may tend toward nonpredictable patterns when an exogenous variable is attended to and adjusted. In a common example, a restaurant may find itself patterned because of the cigarette left in an ashtray. Some theorists call this the *butterfly effect,* by which they have in mind the fact that a single butterfly in a southeast Asian country may flutter about, and this movement may set in motion a typhoon that affects millions of people. Chaos theory is strongly deterministic.

Chaos theorists further postulate that complex structures are by nature *dissipative.* They depend on the initial conditions of the system but over time tend to take unpredictable paths. Unpredictability seems to manifest itself, once the chaotic system is launched, into strange clusters, unusual bloomings, clumps, flows, and trajectories. What had been initial disorder now reveals new and beautiful patterns and harmonies that were undetected in the original (Hofstadter, 1985).

At the heart of much of chaos theory are numerous assumptions about the nature of man, nature, and the universe that are by no means uniformly held. Historically, philosophy had focused on the universe as an orderly *cosmos.* God represented reason and truth. The world he made was therefore orderly. Philosophers and scientists, motivated by their theological beliefs, characterized reality as harmonious and orderly. Although human beings were imperfect and hence could not fully understand this order, it was their duty to attempt to discover God's plan. Aristotle inspired thinkers to seek to discover the order of this cosmos through logical reasoning.

With the modern introduction of inductive scientific method, thinkers such as Thomas Hobbes (*Leviathan,* 1950) and Sir Francis Bacon (*Novum Organum,* 1899) proposed that the investigator was dealing with chaos. Nature was not driven by a single goal. The idea of cosmos was dead. In the place of theologically given harmony was chaos. The role of the researcher was to bring order to this disorder. The tools were empirical study and inductive logic. By collecting many characterizations of a system, the system could be generalized. This iteration and linear tracing forms the capstone of the new science of chaos.

An Analysis of Chaos Theory

Chaos theorists seek a new view of the universe. They reject the cosmic characterization of the ancients. Chaos theory proposes that the universe is ultimately and largely disordered to the point of frenzy. However, at a deeper level, the orderliness tends to be a function of the complexity of the universe as this chaos winds itself out over time. But chaos is reintroduced and reiterated over time. Thus rather than, as Peirce proposed, a universe evolving toward a patterned and more logical order, the entire project is a pulsating chaos-order machine.

The mechanistic metaphor is appropriate. Human intervention is possible, but rational control is not. Thus, the chaos is a given and predetermined state of reality. Nothing humans can do will change the ultimate nature of the universe. Cause and effect accounts are unprofitable because of the complexity of the interactions.

As a counter to this deterministic characterization of the universe, William James proposed that relations between things, linked as well as unlinked, are as much matters of direct particular experience, neither more nor less so, than the things themselves. This pillar of James's "radical empiricism" reintroduced the observer into the meaning equation and removed the "extraneous trans-empirical connective support" (Perry, 1922, pp. x-xi). Transferring this concept to the present issue of whether the institution of the school is chaotic or orderly, we see that the role of the observer is a factor in this determination. The extent to which we may characterize schools as disorderly, fragmented, or fractured is intimately tied to our own direct experience (past and present) of these institutions.

Chaos theory is Calvinism writ large. If we unpack the theory, we find some components are orderly and seem to progress toward a satisfactory station. Other parts of the firmament are subject to dissolution, decay, or disorder. From the outset we do not know which parts of the universe are predestined for strange attractor status or complex patterning and which elements are destined for chaotic disequilibrium and disarray. Calvinism preached this thesis with respect to human salvation.

Most metaphysical philosophers start with a primacy of substance and then attempt to categorize this substance. In the case of chaos theory, the substance is characterized as multileveled, complex, recursive, dissipative, and, above all, disorderly. The explanatory network that is used is thought to be embedded in the substance and revealed through the workings or mechanisms of the substance. The categories themselves are not seen to be in flux but rather operative simultaneously. Characteristics of the field are relative to the condition of the complexity under view and not the instruments used to view it. This assumption is methodological. The instrument used, the framework through which one views the phenomena, reveals what is there. The reality of the substance is naively assumed to be unconnected to either the instruments used or the characteristics of the human observer. Chaos substance is a *reality sui generis* in the sense that it exists irrespective of instruments used to detect it or human limits on observation. The chaos operates according to its own rules, which are above those of culture, society, or human decision.

Chaos theory relies on structure. Chaos is patterned, if in no other way, as unsteady, expansive, irregular, nonlinear, and so forth. Thus the chaos qua chaos is classifiable as unpredictable (the substance is in disarray). But even in its amorphous state, chaos has the potential for order, an order of a new type. Regardless of the mechanism that brings such order (often seen as synonymous with deeper levels of complexity) into being, chaos to order and order to chaos display patterning. The patterning is surprisingly rich in texture. It may well operate like a supersaturated solution, with any additions resulting in the return to solid form. No matter what career the chaos substance follows, it is possible to attribute structure to it. It is this feature of chaos theory that makes it so amendable to structuralist philosophies such as Piaget's developmentalism. In fact, it may be claimed that ontology reiterates cosmology: The individual human organism passes through the chaos-order processes found operative in galactic space.

The effort to read from the cosmos certain formation and deformation rules for individual child development places chaos theory within a group of grand theories such as Herbartianism or Froebelianism. These theories represented the 19th-century effort to explain all processes in children and schooling from a supernatural point of view. Just as Froebel's study of crystals led to extrapolations from crystal-growing experiments to kindergarten teaching and learning proposals, chaos theorists would read off teaching methods from the nature of computer-enhanced mathematical iterations. The crucial question is, How do the transformations of computer screen graphic displays of numeric operations tell us anything at all about how teachers should teach? The universe viewed as chaotic in its essentials need not warrant introducing chaos into the first-grade classroom.

Experience. In place of a metaphysics of chaos-substance, it is possible to speak of a metaphysics of experience. Substance and structure are encountered by human agents as living organisms, as activity. Dewey provided a helpful insight into how to deal with efforts to account for existence as a whole. Humans can encounter the metaphysical only piecemeal and then not as existence (being) but rather as experience. Sleeper (1986, p. 133) cites Sidney Hook's explanation of Dewey's view: "Traditional metaphysics has always been a violent and logically impossible attempt to impose some parochial scheme of values on the cosmos in order to justify or undermine a set of existing social institutions by a pretended deduction from the nature of Reality" (Hook, 1939, p. 3).

Dewey (1926/1958) in *Experience and Nature* noted that the most important category here is one of *transaction*. What we are after when we seek meaning is an account not of being but of experience as transactions between humans and their environs (nature). Metaphysics serves us in a critical pragmatism as it functions to bind together the diverse and conflicting parts of human actions, providing some coherent relation between culture and nature (Sleeper, 1986). The ultimate nature of nature may be at once chaotic and orderly; however, this essential condition calls for human effort to work it out toward some end-in-view. When humans relate to chaos they do so from some praxeological point. *Emancipation* has become a buzz word in education, but it nonetheless points to the acceptance of the fact that human will makes a difference. Chaos theory seems to underestimate human will and to replace it with a transcendent power. We can only watch chaos unfold. The Maginot Line of meaning is breached, and we must wait for the system to run its course. Belief plays a key role here. As Alice James (Barzun, 1983) pointed out, the world does not remember the misery we as individual human beings encountered, but it does record what type of effort we put up against it.

Chaos theory is essentially a species of conflict theory in disguise. If things are ordered—disorder them (i.e., create conflict). Conflict is disagreement, nonconsensus, and dialogic. Confront, contradict, and confuse so that the student will learn. The chaotic state of the universe is seen as warrant for introducing chaos into the classroom. If the natural condition of students is to be in turmoil, the teachers' duty is to dislodge order, linearity, and continuity to return them to their natural state. It is assumed that we learn more from chaos as method than from order. Some people like disorder, thrive on chaos, and must have stress in their lives and work. Adrenalin flows and these sensationalists get "high" on discord. Putting out brush fires and dealing with crises make for administrative success in schooling. Complexity requires professionalism and expertise to deal with it; hence, chaos theory breeds the need for greater administrative or teacher control and power. Chaos theory is the path to a more bureaucratic system because it necessitates a technical expert capable of dealing with large and complex (disorderly) systems.

At the root of chaos theory is an epistemological view that sees knowledge as a positive means of dealing with disorder. It is interesting that chaos theory as a species of educational theory is consensual in the fact that it assumes agreement on the epistemological characterization of the substance and structure of the universe (i.e., we must all agree that things are in disarray), although on the other hand, it introduces cognitive conflict as a way of adjusting students to the chaotic nature of the cosmos. Orderly treatment of claims about chaos is common to the treatment, but consensus seeking within the chaos is discouraged. To so treat knowledge is to see it as dichotomous relative to levels of being.

A "new science of chaos" is a contradiction that poststructuralist science has proposed that the modes of inquiry themselves must be open to scrutiny. Consensus at the level of inquiry theory is opposed to discord at the level of phenomenological operations. Thus, rather than being postmodernist-poststructuralist as claimed, chaos theory of education is conservative, modernist thinking writ large: an effort to engage in a grand narrative.

Applying Chaos Theory to Schools

What began as a marginal and rather insignificant theoretical stance in physics and mathematics has moved to the status of a serious framework of beliefs and experimental findings for a variety of fields of study (Stewart & Golubitsky, 1992). It is not hard to understand the recent adoption of chaos theory by researchers and writers in education. Chaos thinking has become a full-blown theory of education in a few short years.

The fields of curriculum theorizing, in general, and science and mathematics teaching, in particular, have led the effort to extrapolate teaching methods and materials for instruction from chaos theory (Doll, 1993; Oliver & Gershman, 1989). By severely criticizing the modernist characterization of schooling, these curricular postmodernists seek to replace the rational, technical, piecemeal analysis of the problems and prospects of socially construed teaching and learning with some form of curricular thinking and practice more appropriate to the changing times. They call for an essentially conservative postmodern theory of educational discourse and practice that forms a more disciplined study to account for the elements missing from the chaotic landscape of schooling while elevating a single cultural-scientific-metaphysical-religious-historical framework for that purpose. By embracing holistic and cosmological understandings, a new, larger set of warrants for seeing curriculum and pedagogy will emerge, we are told. Because the effort is one of pushing upward toward the more metaphysical and abstract, certain favorable social and pedagogical theorists are appropriated for support. Alfred North Whitehead's process philosophy, John Dewey's experimentalism, Piaget's and Kohlberg's developmentalism, and Bruner's psychology may be expropriated for the task of backing a grand theory of chaos to warrant particular curricula and teaching methods.

New Age and ecological in timbre, the writings in this camp appear to resurrect a type of progressive child-centered romanticism. Chaos as a type of postmodern Disney ride becomes the root metaphor for this new philosophy of education. Ultimately, chaos theory seems to serve as a countermodernist movement. The discourse surrounding what ought to be taught in the schools reacts to the conventional Tyleresque positivism with its emphasis on the three Rs. Emerging from this reactive postmodernism is a radical personalism with overtones of religious redemption. A new school vision is based in a medieval cosmology of determinacy, relativism, and complexity. The unit under scrutiny is the individual child but might just as well be a tree or endangered species. Beneath the surface chaos is a structural and developmental theory of biological change, providing the rationale for biosocial transformation via restructuration. Emphasis is placed on the innate tendency of humans to move toward steady-state reequilibration. Psychophysical realignment is taken here as the device essential for restructuring (forming and transforming) the organism; the teacher's art is one of monitoring, accelerating, and encouraging this transformation.

On the critical side, intercession on the part of the teacher and curriculum may well be problematic for postmodernists fully invested in chaos theory as a psychocosmological grand theory. We cannot read from this chaos or the organic transformations what we ought to do in schools. The problem for such grand theories of cosmological chaos is to provide the middle-range moves. How shall postmodern teachers and curricularists know when and how they must intervene in this essentially superorganic process?

Curriculum chaos theory is currently an eclectic mix of child-centered progressivism, structuralist and Freudian psychology, theological process philosophy, and ecological romanticism. Only in very elliptical ways does the curricular chaos framework match the physics of chaos popularizers Prigogine and Stengers (1984). (Recently, advocates have developed an aversion to the use of the word *chaos*, preferring *disorder*.) In the final analysis, chaos theory, insofar as curricular proposals are concerned, underwrites what is essentially a more inclusive theory of curricular construction and pedagogical intervention than the modernist version, which is diffused over rationalism, technologism, and scientism. Given sufficient time, the chaotic begins to look sublimely ordered; pattern emerges out of mess. A deep and abiding faith in progress, nature, and human psychological readjustment is assumed. Far beneath the surface of this type of curricular recommendation is a sublime faith in superorganic forces that direct and control our human journey. Society is a great and beautiful beast to be tamed not by rationality and control but through faith in nature and its iterations. The theory of conservative postmodern curriculum chaos means we may rest assured that whatever the current chaos, there is a willful and clever force at work, guiding and controlling our destiny.

The Politics of Chaos

The essentially contested issue in chaos theory versus other frameworks is the status of local knowledge over global knowledge (Hayles, 1990). The question emerges of whether or not chaos theory may be a political theory and, perhaps more than this, an ideological position, which entails a metanarrative that resists critique and reconstruction. Bernstein (1983), Foucault (1969/1972), and Rorty (1979) have shown that knowledge tends to be socially constructed; Giroux (1988c), Johnston (1994), McKinney and Garrison (1994), Miron and Elliott (1994), and Stanley (1992) argue that such knowledge requires resistance and reconstruction.

A caution is needed: We must guard against the move toward global theories and ideologies (such as chaos theory) in the face of what are actually practical problems. The abstract principles of chaos theory must press us to adopt a method that allows for theory critique (holds up such principles as testable against practice) while providing a method for their test. By placing practical problems first and ideological or grand frameworks last, we give space to intelligent thought and launch it for the task of reconstructing any position that takes itself as an a priori or absolute while simultaneously offering us techniques of practical judgment to deal with the day-to-day realities of social life.

For critical pragmatism each and every type of human association has a political aspect. Schools are human associations constructed for social purposes. Although the political right favors construing such institutions as arenas of epistemological competition, the critical pragmatic position advanced here sees them as territories of collaboration and cooperation.

Hayles (1990) would have us believe that chaos theory aids us in dealing with problems of scale and thus allows local knowledge to be tethered to grand theory. Her example is the coastline of Britain, which may be viewed at a number of scales, each more detailed. The matter of size is significant here. Someone may wish to purchase a home on a bay but would be unsatisfied if it were only large enough to accommodate a termite. The value of chaos thinking is that it allows us to move between the levels and understand them as elaborations on a theme. The difficulty with this line of thinking is that it overlooks key issues attached to matters of scale.

Thus, although chaos theory may provide explanatory devices regarding the phenomena of schooling, it is insufficient in helping us sort out issues affecting individuals from those families of institutions. The problem for chaos theorists is that they fail to take seriously the problem of the one and the many, as it was termed in ancient philosophy. It cannot account for individuals except as parts of wholes, units, or conglomerates. Individuals are lost, and this disappearance is what prompts the crisis in postmodern thinking in general. Hayles (1990) argued that critical theory finds the claims of the local are unexpanded "until the local itself becomes a new kind of globalizing imperative" (p. 214). But this is to miss the fact that critical theory, unlike chaos theory, seeks to critique rather than shore up global knowledge. Instead of a deductive move, we find an inductive gesture leading to short-termed principles of procedure. The globalization here is never one of resolute "I-told-you-so" but rather one of "what-if?" Thus Hayles has sought to tar critical theory (and I would add critical pragmatism) with the same brush: Both are invested in seeking to globalize knowledge. But this clearly is not the case. In the last analysis, Hayles viewed chaos theory as providing a Russian doll model of the universe wherein local problems-knowings are simple reproductions of larger scaled problems-knowings: They are "images of each other" (p. 219). Holism becomes the ultimate explanatory destiny, and the separation between science and literature is filled in by a new scientism that provides constraints of a physical sort on social discourses and practices. Hayles seems to evidence a socioscientistic penchant to subject all phenomena to physical constraints, but she misunderstands that these are always viewed through her metatheoretical chaos with its absolute principles of unity, symmetry, recursion, and order out of disorder. Following from Hayles's embrace of chaos theory is her application of that theory of physics to literary products. For Hayles, there is no difference between the forces operative on the geography of Britain and the forces affecting a novel or poem.

Chaos and Social Organization

Chaos theorists move easily from their scientific framework to school policy. For example, Marion (1992) found no difference in understanding the mathematics of chaos and the mathematics of social organizations. Chaos theory can explain the complexity of social structures through the scientific investigation of system dynamics. According to Marion:

> If certain behaviors of a social system were quantifiably and continuously monitored over time and plotted on a graph . . . the resultant lines should not settle into a repetitive pattern (simple determinism), nor would they distribute randomly. Rather the plot would detail patterned diversity. The graph would be mathematically stable. . . . The stable element of organizational behavior that is represented by such a plot is constrained by forces such as role expectations, mores and human capability. (p. 169)

Chaos theory allows the researcher to model social systems' behavior so that what appears random behavior of the system is actually "a product of deterministic dynamics . . . yet is eminently complex and unpredictable" (p. 170). A mathematical model of chaos should provide explanations of teaching and learning in the future. As a grand theory of school organization, Marion's chaos vision will account for the predetermined dynamics of all of education through statistical graphs and charts.

Marion claimed that his version of chaos theory strikes a bargain between the pragmatic interactionism of Dewey and Mead and the stability hypothesis of earlier scientists. But to so argue is to misunderstand Dewey and Mead. These pragmatists argued nature is "an affair of affairs" (Dewey, 1926/1958, p. 97) with continuities as well as breaks. Social organizations, following the pragmatic line of thinking, are both chaotic and orderly. In addition, Marion and like-minded chaos theorists overlook humans' freedom of choice. They presume the organization is a predetermined system, controlled by external operating rules. Choices by humans merely deflect the matter in motion: The organizational system is a beautiful kaleidoscope of ever-changing pattern.

In the face of present-day crises in business administration, chaos theory has worked its way into management and organizational theory texts in business schools across the country. Wall Street brokers have come to rely on statistical packages that plot chaos into the vicissitudes of the stock market. Peters (1987) provoked the business leader to learn the art of *Thriving on Chaos*. Bergquist (1993) classified the present situation in business organization as being embedded in a premodern, modern, and postmodern situation. Today's corporations are in trouble because they must recognize their historical forms while envisioning new postmodern cultural requirements needed for success in the future. The chaos faced by organizations must be understood and then navigated if they are to survive.

Yet when we consider the role of individuals in the cosmos, we must move from notions of wholes, collectivities, and aggregates to those of individuals, singularities, and particulars. Juxtaposed against the nation, state, and community as system is the idea of the *self*. Individuals seem to have some bearing on the interrogation of the chaos view. Charles Taylor (1989), in talking of the sources of the self, proposed that the current rejection of objective order has its roots in the modern search for the moral good. Chaos theorists, on this reading, would be positing complexity theses in a mistaken belief that such characterizations reveal the ultimate nature of the universe, although overlooking the place of humankind's centuries-old search for a moral basis for societal forms. The chaos theorists' desire to reestablish the quixotic, short-range explanation of things overlooks the deeper value of the modernist agenda in aligning the individual self with larger human purposes. But Taylor's narrow conclusion that only the modernist agenda is capable of confronting chaos with moral-ethical ideals is an unfair indictment that sweeps together conservative postmodernists embracing chaos theory as well as affirmative postmodernists who retain faith in the power of individuals to freely choose to change society with an eye to a vision of a moral order.

At the same time, we must be on the alert for those individuals who would introduce chaos as a normative moral ideal. It is naive to believe that everyone wishes the best to happen: Were a destructive individual to get his or her way, chaos would be a wonderful device for gaining power. Both William James and Christopher Lasch (1991) have pointed to the insight that it is naive to think that genuine evil does not exist in the world. Chaos, where it is viewed as a positive value, may well represent this evil as an ideal. Charles Manson, the mass murderer, fostered chaos with his helter-skelter philosophy of rape and plunder in southern California. More recently, international terrorism has introduced chaos into travel with the indiscriminate bombing of airplanes. Chaos is upsetting to systems at the simpler level of organization, but chaos provides very real potential for representative evil.

As an educational ideal, chaos theory must be handled with caution. A student struggling with self-concept as well as an understanding of a subject or skill rarely welcomes teacher-induced chaos. Learning seems to entail both organization and reorganization—it seldom prospers under conditions of continuous fracture, discontinuity, and dissolution. The naive notion that students learn "from the simple to the complex" must be rejected; also, the introduction of complexity as the singular teaching process is nonsense as well. Only when we see human interactions (experiences) as combining both order and disorder, with the natural human inclination to move to the simple, are we on the path to correctly dealing with chaos in the classroom. From a classroom organization standpoint, chaos seems a synonym for undisciplined behavior for most teachers. When "chaos reigns," little in the way of instruction is possible. Overly rigid and dictatorial classrooms are not the solution, certainly. However, we must learn to balance rules with creative expression. Having no rules leads to anarchy and chaos in interpersonal relations; totally rule-governed behavior results in stifling innovation.

There is a penchant for orderly discourse in chaos theory that overrides the anarchistic nature of the universe these theorists seek to report. Although the cosmic heavens may be in disarray and complex beyond our efforts to understand, this narrative assertion is not. We thus have introduced a dualism between cosmos and narrative: the one disorderly, the other orderly. We have replaced our dichotomy between orderly and disorderly worlds with order as a linguistic reality versus cosmic immaterial-material reality.

One of the many difficulties with chaos theory may be the result of its being a grand theory. Entailing claims about the ultimate nature of the universe, the unseen character of transformations, and the assumptions regarding free will and determinism are problematic because ordinary mortals cannot find a perch from which to view the show. Pegging our pedagogical practice to theories of the universe releases us from the responsibility for constructing worthwhile middle-range theories that help make sense of day-to-day difficulties we face in our institutions. A critically pragmatic reconceptualization of chaos theory may amount to nothing more than substituting a process that divorces all grand theory from practical decision making. If we focus on teaching acts, for example, we may wonder what practical difference theoretical chaos physics may make for teachers engaged in particular acts of teaching. Where no difference can be detected in how we teach children, we may choose to jettison chaos theory.

Beyond Chaos and Structure

What would schools and teaching look like were we to abandon the cosmological framework of mainstream chaos theory? It is possible to draw on a critical pragmatism to interrogate the concepts of organization and chaos with the intention of generating a more adequate philosophy of school reordering.

In nature we find clusters of flowers, assemblies of electrons, swarms of insects, flocks of birds, herds of cattle, and constellations of stars. Schools are sites of associated living, distinctly plural and often complex. Collectivities are discernable throughout nature. As John Dewey argued in *The Public and Its Problems* (1927/1946), the difficulty is not so much how an individual becomes part of the collectivity but what distinguishes human associations from other forms of grouping. The answer seems to lie in the fact that consequences of association may be traced by humans. According to Dewey, associated behavior is "directed toward objects which fulfill wants" (p. 106).

Human-associated behavior produces objects that also yield sociocultural customs and traditions. Beyond this, when the ends and results of association in action are intelligently and emotionally appreciated (valued), a shared interest results. This common interest has an effect on the interconnected behavior so that it becomes changed. When the consequences of collective action are realized, the recognition of these gains tends to transform the conditions from which the behavior and acting arose (Dewey, 1927/1946).

As humans join in collective action, they tend to reflect on the association itself. Hence we find forms of association such as school organizations drawing our attention. Every person acts when she or he recognizes the connection with the group. Individual persons think and plan, but what they think and plan is the outcome of their behavior as a part of the collectivity (Dewey, 1927/1946). We may have a variety of motives for joining a group; however, these associated forms of living have a critical importance to school reformers. Whatever members may think or do, these matters become objects of critique as they emerge from the interactions within the association.

A critical pragmatic perspective on the nature of schools must not assume such forms of social aggregation are givens, as chaos theorists lead us to believe. Dewey (1927/1946) stressed again and again that human individuals never join together into social groups by mere chance or accident. Rather, human associations, such as schools, develop into social groups as their achievements are esteemed and sought after.

Chaos theorists building on the psychological theories of Piaget or Kohlberg or on the political views of Hobbes or Locke assume that humans join together and form societies because of a clustering instinct. Efforts to explain human social association according to instincts such as gregariousness or the struggle for survival and search for power explain everything—yet nothing. Impulses, drives, and instincts are actually shaped by the same social conditions they are seen to create (Dewey, 1927/1946).

Pragmatic explanations of institutions such as schools reject the historical efforts to root such characterizations in grand theories that simultaneously neglect the empirical facts of human collective existence. Following Dewey's lead, it may be argued that studies of school restructuring must begin with observations of actual associated behavior in schools. We need studies of schools that debunk historical and logical efforts to read key variables from antecedent abstractions of educational association, seeking to match these as dependent and independent in character. Shotter (1993) made an effort to cut through such abstractions in characterizing such searches as investigations into "the cultural politics of everyday life," coming to understand how we act "from within" a cultural space made up of human experiences (p. xiii).

Organization and Structure

Although the term *organization* continues to operate in discourse as an abstract collective noun (*reorganization* providing the action form of the word) and *structure* and *restructure* take on an analogous position in the rhetoric, there are distinctions to be made. *Organization* should be seen as a mechanism by which the collectivity operates. Organization is the process of forming or ordering. However, it has taken on a modernist meaning that translates into coordinating or connecting the parts into some constituted body—managing. Once the elements are linked and coordinated, the associated collectivity may be termed an organization.

Structure is an arrangement of parts or elements, a type of framework or scaffolded construct that contains parts or elements related in some way(s), as opposed to *disorganized* (having the elements in disarray). However, being structured and unstructured does not imply the same disordering: The latter implies that the parts are evident but are not tiered or layered. *Restructuring* assumes a reestablishment of structure, a type of reallocation of the elements in arrangement. Where we find proposals to restructure schools, we must be on the alert for efforts to reimpose the prior arrangements that have weakened or fallen into disarray. Attached to such proposals may be the assumption that all we must do is "fix" the schools by repairing the structure.

Reorganization seems to run afoul of somewhat similar difficulties. When we reorganize, we are attempting to reconnect the elements, form new interdependencies, and coordinate pieces in new ways. It is assumed that the formation of relationships of parts and processes are in need of systematic reordering. For example, infantry in battle who have suffered a setback are encouraged (commanded) to reorganize behind the lines and try again. So too, we find school reformers who have in mind reorganization as reenforcing units and/or reestablishing chains of command. Currently large industries in the United States are reorganizing by cutting out layers of middle management. The resulting structure is one that is "lean and mean" and "cost-effective." This approach is applauded by many restructurers who are interested in streamlining management in the schools, too.

There is a wide variety of human associations, the school being one type. However, all associations have in common the fact of intermember relations. We often overlook the fact that schools are social sites filled with active and growing children and adults. Structures are frames and skeletons on which we must hang our ideational sheeting and flooring—they invite connecting and coordinating. Viewed from the frameworks perspective, the problem of school restructuring is a problem of links and coupling. Pragmatism tells us that even more critical is the understanding of human meanings. We must get these meanings straight if we are to succeed in reforming education.

Clearly, we must admit that not all associated forms of life, including schools, are good. Gangs of thieves and groups of thugs and vandals come to mind as evil or bad. It is entirely possible for individual students, teachers, and administrators to become part of a school that finds conditions circumscribing action and controlling or stultifying participation. Organization is the mechanism through which associations operate. Tightly coupled or structured schools tend to limit the choices and alternatives available to members; loosely coupled schools may provide greater alternatives for human action.

Individuals and Individualism

In the 1920s and 1930s America witnessed social and political movements that pragmatists came to regard as detrimental to individuals (Dewey, 1930). Through the rise of a new corporate and external model of business and industrial organization, individual workers came to lose their individuality. But there were two sides to this coin. On one side was the notion of rugged individualism, praised by the giants of industry as the motive beneath the corporate scheme to achieve dominance at the expense of the worker. Strikes and violence resulted from this external notion of individualism. Dewey proposed on the other side that a superior mode of organization could be adopted. Needed was an internal mode of organization, one that bred the qualities of life overlooked in the first.

Although the external form of corporate organization had been unreflective and integrationist, mechanical and quantitative, Dewey envisioned an arrangement that took into consideration changes in American culture. Dewey (1930) really envisioned what may be called a postmodern culture emerging in the first half of the 20th century. Human associations within this new culture were quantitatively and qualitatively different. New modes of communication and travel prompted the rise of new forms of association. The individual human being had to be viewed differently. Dewey warned that "while individuals are now caught up into a vast complex of associations, there is no harmonious and coherent reflection of the import of these connections into the imaginative and emotional outlook on life" (p. 82).

Dewey felt that the mechanical integration of American social and cultural organization was a large part of the problem of democracy in the 1930s. American society had been forced into a state of economic integration in which a few wealthy and powerful individuals controlled the lives of the masses. Needed in the place of social chaos was a way of associated life that was open, strong, stable, flexible, and free.

Pragmatists in the first half of this century saw a social and cultural crisis as a function of modernism that is not very different from our own situation. Today we see a pluralistic culture of complexity and confusion. Postindustrial and postmodern in nature, this culture is assumed to be a fertile field for restructuring and reorganization. But just as Dewey had warned in the 1930s, the problem is deeper than the old frameworks seem to imply. Just as industrialization would not automatically produce a new culture for our forefathers, today postindustrialism has no potential to yield a new culture either.

The key, which Dewey as a critical pragmatist saw, was that to achieve a genuine and good society and culture it was necessary to wrestle the general culture and society away from old forms of organization. For us, it is necessary to take back control of our own institutions from those who would convert them into images of organization long in the tooth. Only by freeing the intelligence and refining the emotions of individuals will we be able to do so (Dewey, 1930). Much has been written of the pragmatist's interest in solidarity (Rorty, 1989). Human sociocultural associations require individualism, however, not at the expense of cooperation and mutual recognition. Although industrialism and postindustrialism have placed the responsibility for organizational reform in the hands of certain elite individuals, reform must be seen as the prerogative of the many. Implicit in a critical pragmatic view of school reform is the notion that it must proceed from the bottom up because of the nature of our culture and the types of associated living deemed important.

Conclusions

In some sense the answer to the question of how chaos theory will affect schooling theory and practice has already been assumed. Educational researchers are beginning to move from positivistic mind-sets to more open naturalistic and qualitative research methods. One interesting example of this shift speaks to the controversy between the chaos theorists and other postmodern-poststructuralist theorists: School research has begun to abandon the notion that global frameworks reveal differences in schooling across nations and states. It is being argued that research must be conducted at the level of individual schools because each school is so different from every other that comparison between them is nearly impossible. The tendency is to move from the global characterization of school effects to localized generalizations. In some measure this refocus on more local forms of knowledge about schooling is a result of the realization that critical aspects of individual schools must be captured if we are to know how to fix education. Differences between schools are seen as tied to differences in the local school space and its children, teachers, parents, and administrators who interact within it.

The upshot of this more localized thinking and research is that educational chaos is now believed to be less generalized than at first thought. Rather than seeing chaos in entire nations, researchers are arguing that within these entities lie orderly and effective individual schools that are succeeding. Were we to propose a model for the new school order, it would be one in which local differences in schools, with attention to children's experiences, are to be encouraged rather than expunged. Such thinking flies in the face of traditional bureaucratic statistical conceptions of public education.

Certainly, the more popular claim for reforming schooling has rested on the assumption that the universe is rationally ordered. Because everything is ordered in the universe (a variety of the Great Chain of Being argument), then this school or this educational system also must be ordered. The bulk of educational management books assume this orderly world view. They induct succeeding generations of principals and superintendents into the naive belief system that has perpetuated the difficulties found in our institutions today. Chaos theory as applied to organizations such as schools sought to confront the modernist and rational characterization of such conglomerates. However, the practical consequence has been to reintroduce a conservative and stable underlying order to such organizations. Rather than engaging in postmodern-poststructural and critical efforts to understand schools, chaos theory has served a modernist and structuralist set of explanations. Curriculum, teaching, and school administration all have felt the effect of this move toward organizational stability and control.

This chapter has contended that embracing chaos theory as explanatory for school restructuring is an effort at grasping at metaphysical straws. The nature of the universe is a long-standing concern of philosophers, but the question whether it is chaotic or orderly has not been answered in all the centuries intelligent beings have wondered. We would be ill-advised to attempt to read the rationale for reordering schooling from a metaphysical and cosmological guess.

I have argued for the concept of human association and individual experience over that of organization and structure as the primary unit of sociocultural cluster. Associated action is natural and universal. Such action has results, some of which are perceived in the sense that they are taken account of with the result that designs and plans come to be prized and a common interest in them generated. At this juncture, two different types of interests and regulative means are open to us: Either (a) the interest and control of actions are limited only to the few directors, managers, and administrators or (b) the control and measurement are extended to participants in the actions to which the group is dedicated. In the former case, robber barons and industrial giants have dominated the corporate organization to the detriment of the workers. In the latter case, we witness the team leadership and individual on-the-line decisions of the newer forms of industrial organization from Volvo to Honda.

School restructuring must take into consideration the basic nature of culture and society, develop reform strategies cognizant of these configurations, and seek to improve the overall good for persons and community. Suggestions as to how this may be done have been offered in this chapter; however, the fuller understanding of the role of school reformers and chaos-order requires an understanding of the nature of democracy.

The next chapter explores the relationship between the chaos-order debates and democracy as a form of school redesign. In the pages to follow I will propose that democracy provides the best sociopolitical arrangement for schools as we seek to reconstruct our American way of life.

3

স্থ

Democracy and
Educational Organizations

Democracy

The meanings of democracy are so varied that political regimes from
the most authoritarian to the most anarchistic invoke the term in their
self-descriptions. Anyone may use the word *democratic* to explain
organization. However, for societies invested in the belief that individuals have the right to govern themselves, democracy has taken
on an importance that demands it be dealt with in any consideration
of institutional arrangement and organization. This is no less true
of schools today as they embark on educational reforms of the most
sweeping sort.

The Two Liberalisms

Liberal democracy has had the most effect on Western nations,
and this version of democracy continues to dominate thinking today
as we wrestle with upheavals in our society. There have been several
historical versions of liberalism over the centuries, but the essential

contest is between early 20th-century modern liberalism and what this book shall argue for, a new postmodern liberalism for the 21st century.

Modern liberalism conceived of a society in which the emphasis was on private individuals. Institutions of government were means by which these isolated individuals were governed by elected representatives. This modernist form of democracy was pluralistic and relativistic. The public interest was taken to be the sum total of all individual interests, forming an endless calculation of self-interest (Anderson, 1990; Dryzek, 1990).

Postmodern liberalism emphasizes the cooperative nature of organized human experience and uses certain value criteria for choosing the better and distinguishing it from the worst. The democratic value structure is not so much rooted in some set of external principles as it is a middle-range group of regulative norms. Metanarrative notions warranting democracy as a rational-technical ideal may be replaced with commitments to new pragmatic norms to authenticate democratic choosing. These democratic values are (a) the belief in the worth and dignity of individuals and the value of their expressions and participation; (b) the reverence for freedom, intelligence, and inquiry; and (c) the responsibility of individuals in concert to explore and choose collaborative and communal courses of practical action. These norms arise as values to be achieved rather than ideals guaranteed in advance. As deliberative criteria these values are located in the historical and developing experiences of people and in their institutions. The norms outlined here are essential to our understanding of how democracy and school reform must fit together if we are to see education prospering into the 21st century.

Incidentally, it is no surprise these democratic values are part of pragmatic philosophy. Democracy forms the context in which children and youth derive the richest possibilities for growing into successful individuals. Schools reconstructed on democratic lines provide the best form of associated intelligent and aesthetic living.

It is necessary to distinguish two forms of postmodernism operative today—skeptical postmodernism and affirmative postmodernism (Rosenau, 1992). First, skeptical postmodernism views with suspicion democracy as representation. Skeptical postmodernists tend to be nihilistic, negative, and despairing about organizations. It is their perception that the mass media have manipulated democratic forms of life (Baudrillard, 1993). For skeptical postmodernists, representative government has failed to accurately reflect the wishes of the masses of people (Rosenau, 1992).

Affirmative postmodernists, although critical of democracy and representation, seek to replace representation with more local and freer forms of human expression. More direct forms of democracy that stress grassroots and local participation are substitutes for modernist democracy. Democracy must be deepened. Attached to this reconceptualization of democracy is a critique of authority and leadership. Antielitist, antimanagerial, and antibureaucratic, affirmative postmodernists substitute moral-ethical rectitude, aesthetic creativity, and participation for political formalism, organizational structuralism, and voter representation.

Prevailing methods of policy making and policy analysis incorporate the belief that people should view the choices to be made, study the appropriate consequences, and exercise their responsible preference. Consensus that includes the widest possible range of choosers is best. But beyond the belief in equity and sharing are the first-order demands for cogent understanding of what the problems may be. The fundamental belief in freedom serves as the rationale for discerning a world of unknowns. We are free as participants in a democracy to choose from a range of alternatives. None of these features of democracy implies the use of indoctrination because the new order is neither known nor predictable. The universe is manifestly open textured with a variety of options forming the realized goods.

There is a logical relationship between democracy as a form of social and political life and the institution of the school. Early liberal conceptions of democracy such as Thomas Jefferson's entailed the assumption that for democracy to work as a political system, the vast masses of people must be educated so they could make choices. Attached to this view was the idea that reasonableness could be attained through education. Hence the school became an arm of the political state as it prepared children and youth for later citizenship in the democracy. John Dewey (1916a) wrote of this logical arrangement. The fundamental assumption here was that for democracy to succeed, Americans required a free system of public schools, and for schools to succeed, the context of the institution needed to be a democratic atmosphere for learning. Today, it is significant to ask how schools as organizations in a democratic society should relate to the larger political culture.

Traditionally, the view that schools in democracies must represent democratic values and methods has led to a related question: How much democracy is necessary and sufficient to provide the principled continuity of the system while allowing for the maximum democratic participation of the human beings involved? The institution of the school provides a test case for this concern. Two major stances exist. First, those I shall call the democratic *maximalists* assert that most schools display insufficient amounts of democracy in practice. They point to the lack of parental say in school policy, the voicelessness of students, and the powerlessness of teachers. Democracy requires institutions to be arranged in certain ways, they argue. Distinct versions of democracy—for example, democracy as a social way of living as popularized by John Dewey—necessitate that institutions be organized around human interests, maximize freedom, and grow out of the collective ends of the group and the means selected to achieve group ends.

Second, a group of thinkers I refer to as *minimalists* argue that democracy cannot be extended fully into classrooms without risk. Imposition is required if the principles of democracy, as part of the larger societal values, are to be passed on to uninitiated students. Some minimalists point out that expertise nullifies the rights of the untrained in the decision-making processes. They offer as an example the restriction of the mentally ill or prison inmates in such choice-making processes.

This second group has dominated our history. At least since the rise of the common school in the first half of the 19th century, the fundamental democratic principle of freedom of choice never extended down to our schools. Horace Mann and the early school reformers set up a bureaucratic administrative hierarchy that made certain that students did not choose their teachers, teachers had no say in selection of their principals, and principals had no voice in who would serve as superintendent. Parents were not to determine which school their children would attend. Despite efforts to reform it, the institution of the school to this day is not noted for its democratic character—at least not in the classic meaning of that term.

Contemporary calls for educational change reflect this minimalist versus maximalist controversy. Vouchers, site-based management, teacher empowerment, and other efforts all aim at maximizing the democratic dimension of schooling. Principal academies, certification and licensure, testing of teachers, and other credentialing efforts seek to restrict the voice of those out of power. Although both sides admit the importance of democracy in schools, the type and amount of internal democracy, and with it the type of leadership that is important for a school, are open to question.

Democratic minimalists argue that if the ideal school is not a mirror image of the ideal democratic state, it is because the school must prepare children for the type of citizenship that exists in that state. Children do not come to the school with such skills. Thus minimalists must argue paradoxically that schools may use non-democratic means for inculcating democratic values.

Maximalists, such as John Dewey, believed that a school should be an embryonic and miniature community, purged of the evils of its larger relative. The University of Chicago Laboratory School under Dewey's direction allowed for large democratic participation. Dewey valued shared leadership, treated the teachers as colleagues, and met with them weekly to discuss curriculum and other matters. All teachers had a planning period each day during which they discussed teaching and curriculum ideas with one another. Although students did not have the same control over curriculum or teaching, they did engage in community discussions regarding learning, extracurricular activities, and issues affecting their school. The democratic school elicited a commitment to learning and cultivated democratic virtues among its students. Thus schools that are most internally democratic seem to balance leadership and human participation with the disciplinary purposes of education (Gutmann, 1987).

Authoritarian regimes are fundamentally composed of power and force. Democracies, on the other hand, must focus on questions of choice if they are to avoid repression and silence. Once choice has become central (as it is in democratic ways of life), the processes by which choices become informed and enriched are crucial. Jefferson argued that education was important because informed citizens made the best choosers. The maximization of democracy is thus warranted on the grounds that reasoned deliberation is enhanced by the skills and information derived from education. An educated electorate is seen as essential to the propagation of the democratic state. John Dewey was perhaps the most outspoken proponent of the importance of education for democracy. In *Democracy and Education* (1916a) he pointed out that schools needed to be free and open institutions. Schools themselves had to be democratic if they were to teach children and youth to engage in discussion and to exercise democratic choice. On the other hand, political democracies were the very best systems because they allowed for the fullest type of free schools.

Postliberal Democratic Values

Worth and Dignity of the Individual

Human nature is determined by and in turn controls the environment. The notion that a select superior few, because of inherent natural gifts, are endowed with the ability or right to control the conduct of others, is rejected. Strongly antiauthoritarian, Dewey (1937) asserted that "men's minds and feelings are still permeated with ideas about leadership imposed from above, ideas that developed in the long history of mankind" (p. 458).

Expression. Belief in equality means social organizations provide equality of treatment. Dewey (1937) found that in institutional settings, individuals have an equal right of expression and judgment, although the weight of this judgment "may not be equal in amount when it enters into the pooled result to that of others." Also, the requirement for equality of opportunity comes about because of the unequal distribution of natural and psychological factors (pp. 458-459).

What emerged as problematic for modernist liberalism was the extent to which individuals were seen to participate equally in their own governance. In the wake of the Depression in America, a group of political theorists and politicians recognized the fact that certain groups had been suffering and were without voice in the governing processes. They began espousing a form of democracy that sought representation for and realignment of "the forgotten man." However, through mechanisms of indoctrination and intimidation, social reforms were instituted, creating demigods and dictators.

One of the best examples of this populist democracy gone awry was the political regime of Louisiana's Huey Long, popularized by Robert Penn Warren in his novel *All the King's Men* (1946). Governor Long was committed to retaining power as the political leader at all costs. Machiavellian in technique, Long curtailed public discussion, communication, and community. He developed a hierarchical structured government machine built on deal making and graft. Through his "share the wealth" program, he sought to convince the voters that his goal of "every man a king" could be achieved. Instead, he stole from the rich and gave to the poor but skimmed the richest share for himself and his friends. Coming into power in an oil-rich state, he capitalized on the desires of the land-hungry oil companies to drill and capture Louisiana's resources. Political hegemony was built and maintained. Manipulative and deceptive, Long exercised raw power over the people of Louisiana, intimidated the individual who disagreed with him, used his executive might to cower the legislature and citizens of the state, and ran an oligarchy from the capital until he was assassinated. Long seems to be proof positive that Michels (1959) was correct in charting the logical development of any democracy into an oligarchy of privilege and power.

Participation. There is renewed interest in participatory democracy. Dryzek (1990) argued that participatory democracy rests on reasoning and collaboration. His model of participatory democracy emphasizes communicative rationality and problem solving. Debate grows out of disagreements. Reasoning about and toward public interests and actions takes place within the political communities. Participants govern themselves. Participatory democracy as a form of democracy is best suited for small-scale, geographically bounded units (such as workplaces or neighborhoods) but can work for larger units as well.

For Dewey (1937), democracy's influence on education meant that the formation of the controlling aims, methods, and materials of the schools must be placed in the hands of teachers or their representatives. Where schools were arranged in an authoritarian manner, with teachers playing no role in decision making, teachers would be apt to treat their own students in an autocratic manner.

Dewey (1937) countered two prevalent positions. One view held that teachers were not ready to assume the responsibilities of participation in school leadership. The second view was that through some mysterious mechanism such as natural selection, the "best" people were placed in positions of authority already. Dewey countered by saying that not until teachers were actually given the opportunity to participate in school governance could they assume the responsibility to govern. Dewey believed that teachers could learn to make decisions only by engaging in decision-making practice. Given a pragmatic account of democratic school organization, the best way to produce initiative and constructive power was to practice. Teaching the young as a process could not be understood unless teachers shared in forming the guiding ideas for the school. Teachers were in constant and direct contact with students, although administrators were at their best in indirect contact. Dewey reasoned that what was missing was teacher-to-teacher contact in which they could pool ideas relating to methods and results. Adopting an efficiency argument, he asserted that to deny this cooperative effort was to promote waste. Schools being democratically organized meant for Dewey the application of democracy to everyone in the school.

Participation, Dewey pointed out, is a form of transaction that may be public or private. Those actions that affect only individuals directly engaged in them are private; those actions having consequences for persons not immediately concerned in them are public in character (Westbrook, 1991). The fullest meaning of democracy is that of more than a political arrangement or a slogan such as "one person, one vote." This meaning of democracy spreads beyond the confines of social arrangement or political system.

Discussion. Dryzek's (1990) maximalist democracy "is woven here from threads supplied by a classical (Aristotelian) model of politics, participatory democracy, communicative action, practical reason, and critical theory" (p. ix). Discursive democracy is proposed as a solution to contemporary crises in which democracy, rationality, politics, and policy come together. Echoing Dewey, Dryzek embraces political science but not in an objectivist fashion. He holds that reason must be "critical oversight and discursive meta-design" (p. 219). It follows that discussions of policies calling for school restructuring ought not to be left to elite experts but rather must take place within a public sphere. The instruments and methods are to be evaluated relative to how well they further "discourses of unco-erced communication" (p. 219). The goal for Dryzek is a communi-catively rational, in the sense of interactive, process.

Dewey (1937) stressed the discursive and participatory forms of democratic organization: "The keynote of democracy as a way of life may be expressed, it seems to me, as the necessity for the participa-tion of every mature human being in formation of the values that regulate the living of men together." He went on to say, "all those who are affected by social institutions must have a share in produc-ing and managing them" (pp. 457-458). Silencing voices and exclud-ing people from participation is a subtle form of suppression. It prevents individuals from reflecting on and deciding about the means and methods through which they may gain the enjoyment of what is good for them. Human beings may well be unaware that they have a claim to the development of their own powers. As a result, individuals as well as the entire social body suffers.

Finally, democracy as discursive and participatory is more than political; it is "a way of life." John Dewey (1937) wrote:

> The political and governmental phase of democracy is a means, the best means so far found, for realizing ends that lie in the wide domain of human relationships and the development of human personality . . . It is as we often say, though perhaps without appreciating all that is involved in the saying, a way of life, social and individual. (p. 457)

Freedom-Intelligence-Inquiry

Freedom. Maximalist postliberal participatory democracy rests solidly on the value of freedom—not so much as freedom of action as of freedom of mind. Strongly influenced by Darwinian science, 20th-century pragmatists valued freed intelligence rather than the freedom to do as one pleased. The Bill of Rights sets forth this intellectual freedom (Dewey, 1937).

Intelligence. The agency of human intelligence is the best way to solve the problems confronting societies. Reflective thinking and practical judgment are two characterizations of the type of intellectual arm required for democracy. The emphasis is on critique and choice of a practical type. Judgments are required that resolve problematic situations. Schools are seen as the training ground for such intelligence, and curriculum and teaching form the means by which such critical thought is developed.

Inquiry. To actively live and work in an environment that is democratic requires that we inquire into our difficulties. A democratic form of life rests on a full and free investigation into the sources of information, on the open discussion of issues, and on publication of such information.

What method(s) shall be employed in examining schools as organizations? Experiences of an inquiry type are found within two distinct environments: On the one hand, the environment of authoritarianism locates intelligence in an elite group of decision makers, insulated from the communal intelligence of followers. On the other hand, democracy entails an authority of open inquiry that is shared. To succeed, democracy needs free and open communication among individuals. As Jefferson proposed, the widest community must be literate and ought to engage in study of the problems and options for solution. Certainly there are differences in competing groups and their values and interests; however, via democratic discourse-practice, both authority and decision making are shared. The reconfigured school may well prosper under this regimen.

The shared experiences of the community, the free and open conversations of the largest number of affected members of that community, and the competent inquiry into the problems besetting the group are enablements for the proper conduct of a democratic restructuring effort. In essence, the freedom to inquire and the authority of the group provide a means for planning the new school. The democratic value structure helps community members to realize enriched living through a control of organization and process.

Education is thus a backdrop for democracy as well as the means for continuing the fruitful reconstruction of democracy's institutions.

When considering the mechanisms of choice in a democratic organization, we must take on the mechanisms of thought deemed appropriate to the resolution of problems. For those of us interested in school redesign, pragmatic deliberation is not so much justifying past forms of school structure, critiquing practice against our preferred principles, producing better designs for school organization, and bringing contesting parties to consensus but rather probing the problems of school restructuring with an eye to practical solutions likely to stem from alternative reasonings for change. Our duty as critical pragmatists is to keep the argument open, the dialogue continuous, the interests released, and heretofore silent voices amplified (Anderson, 1990; Bernstein, 1983; Rorty, 1979). Rather than presuming to settle matters, the most important work for critical pragmatism in the democratic reform of schooling is to provide courageous leadership and balance to the discourse-practice relative to educational reconstruction.

Community

In the 1930s wars were fought over what *collectivization* meant. The fundamental and overlooked questions were (a) Will the new societies form into natural aggregates based on the fundamental realization of natural law? or (b) Shall nascent communities arise from the planned staging of a reconstruction and reterritorialization of the material circumstances of human existence? The answer to the first, following an essentially Rousseauian position and, more recently, Alan Bloom's (1987), was yes. There are sufficiently powerful forces in nature and human intelligence to drive us toward the good, if we do not thwart them. Such a social philosophy is optimistic on the one hand because it sees human beings as good by nature but pessimistic on the other hand because of the poor track record of society and political democracies in general and philosophers and humanists in particular in achieving the good society. Bloom suggested that a mirror is required that is made up of great books to see ourselves as we are today and to transform ourselves into the type of citizens that are required for the good society.

Richard Bernstein (1983) provided an affirmative answer to alternative (b) when he found humans on a type of threshold of a renaissance in philosophy in which the philosopher may come to be a cultural critic offering perspective rather than truth. Bernstein spoke of a telos or vision—one of local forms of dialogical community life. Human beings, it is assumed, can be moral, civil, and intellectual. Dialogical communities have as their goal individual human beings participating and providing mutual recognition. Through the everyday practices of dialogue, conversation, phronesis, practical discourse, and judgment, the goal of communal solidarity and unity would be sought.

The irony of both Bloom's and Bernstein's solutions is that they presuppose the type of community they envision as enabling the realization of their vision. We require microsocietal units already practicing Rousseauian naturalism or dialogical praxis in order to bring these types of community into being. Although this essential contradiction seems disabling at first, the sociofuturistic philosopher of education well knows that the first step in becoming what you aspire to be is to purchase the uniform. By the daily habitual practice, you will become what you aspire to be.

Viewed from a critical pragmatic standpoint, community forms the matrix on which bottom-up reforms are to be initiated. If we accept democracy as naming a type of participative life that is at once reflective and reformist in nature, we are on the road to empowerment of local sources of social and cultural reconfiguration.

Chaos and Democracy

Democracy and chaos are closely related. Democracy assumes that the human experience is not preset and may very well be chaotic at times. Although there is a variety of meanings of democracy, each definition embraces freedom of choice. And such choices result from unpredictable states of affairs emerging in the order-chaos of day-to-day living. Power and authority vested in people propel choice in the face of an imperfect and imprecise world. We should not ground our organizational operating system on some abstract cosmology.

Naturalism

The pragmatic perspective offered here rests on naturalism. For John Dewey, the universe was wide open and the course of events was contingent, not predetermined by antecedent forces of either a material or spiritual type. Nature had preference for neither good nor bad. When Dewey's naturalism is traced to his educational philosophy, we find him seeking a reconstructionism of mind, nature, and the world. He proposed that problems were best solved by the method of intelligence. Children in schools should be taught how to control their environment. Because education was a social process, schools should help the child learn to act as part of the group.

When applied to educational organizations, Dewey's experimental naturalism included an acceptance of an evolution in which human reason and morals evolved. Human thought processes emerged in the course of natural activities. For Dewey, mind was a quality of behavior, not given at birth but rather developed. Meaning came when the child, through the mechanisms of habit and experience, affixed meaning to a thing or action. The child made his or her own meanings in the process of learning to participate in living. Thinking was experiencing. Dewey's agenda for experimental naturalism was both the reconstruction of mind and the reconstruction of nature and the world.

In *Experience and Nature*, Dewey (1926/1958) called nature an "affair of affairs" (p. 97). He saw nature consisting primarily of *transactions*. There were three levels of transactions: (a) physiochemical (which the physical sciences investigate); (b) psychophysical (need-demand-satisfaction); and (c) mental, or human experience that is given meaning through language. The differences in these levels were explained by increasing complexity and intimacy of the transactions among natural events, functions, and consequences. A situation or experience is defined by the degree to which it is saturated by a pervading quality. Dewey argued that experience is a method and not a distinctive subject matter. We are told to use the method of experience to make a naturalistic theory of existence, thus bridging naturalism and empirical method. The end product would be a philosophy.

Democracy and School Design

The Politics of Disequilibrium

Two polaristic options have historically set the stage for human choice and organizational structuring: order and disorder. On the side of order have been the classic school reformers such as Horace Mann and Henry Barnard, who fashioned state school systems in the first half of the 19th century to provide greater equality of educational delivery. On the side of disorder have been thinkers such as Thomas Jefferson, who advanced the interests of the "across the mountain people" so that they too (along with the wealthy) could advance their talented youth through schooling.

Leadership in these two views functions quite differently. For the order advocate, leaders need to be strong figures with vision; for the disorder-oriented thinker, leadership is collaborative, fleeting, transitional, and ad hoc.

Democracy, given the two polaristic views of metaphysical structure, is quite variable in its meaning. Robert Michels (1959), for example, argued that it was people's nature to crave or desire power. Once power was achieved, humans sought to perpetuate it. Democracy was thus defined as a form of social organization that led inevitably to oligarchy. Fear of disorder was paramount for Michels. Crowds of people were subject to irrational behaviors. Large political parties lost their democratic principles, and equality was left behind. With the division of labor came specialization and experts. Michels argued that experts, although ostensibly empowered to serve the interests of the organization, quickly developed interests of their own. The logical consequence of this development of professional expertise was bureaucratic organization. Political service became separated from the very interests it proposed to serve (Zeitlin, 1968).

By extrapolating Michels's theory of democracy-oligarchy to the state of schools in America, it is possible to explain the present thrust for decentralized, autonomously run schools. Although the initial tendency has been to seek a democratic voice for the interests of parents and children, the school organization may call on experts to aid in reallocating resources (decentralizing, opening up choice in institutions, etc.). Eventually, these experts will develop an agenda of their own that will lead to a tyranny of small groups of elites over the masses of parents and children.

Economic Individualism

According to educational theorists Chubb and Moe (1990), schools need greater freedom of choice. Parents should be given the right to choose the schools their children attend. However, to accomplish this goal, schooling must be reconfigured into decentralized organizational units, and individual school administrators must be invested with greater autonomy. At the top of the enemies list for such choice theorists are bureaucracy, centralization, and control. We are led to believe that by replacing these foes, we will enable greater democracy. Beneath this argument lurks the economic theory of the free market economy and the politics of disequilibrium.

Assumed in the democratic model advocated by Chubb and Moe (1990) is the fundamental belief in the competitive market nature of democracy. The social and political arrangements are driven by competition. Thus it is logical for Chubb and Moe to see the tare by which we weigh the success or failure of schools as that of production of certain outcomes. Test scores are the surest way of evaluating such outcomes. When test scores go down, the organized nature of schooling is questioned.

Further, by providing parents with vouchers with which they can purchase schooling for their children, schools will be forced to compete. It is assumed parents will choose the best options for their children. Once the market forces are applied to public education, competing institutions will be pressured to improve or be driven out of the educational shopping mall.

The Pluralistic Nature of Democracy and School Organization

What shall be the position played by the individual's interests in a democratic arrangement of social and political life? And on the other side of the ledger, what shall be the public interest?

Democracy may be screened on culture in other ways. Putnam and Putnam (1993) found in Dewey's conception of democracy a justification for a multiculturalism in teaching that prepares children for citizenship in a pluralistic culture. They argued that some versions of multiculturalism do not do this. Putnam and Putnam concluded that respect for other cultures and an interest in promoting and sustaining conversations across ethnic and other lines are essential. According to Rosenthal (1986):

> Dewey stresses that democracy is not a particular body of institutions or a particular form of government, but the political expression of the functioning of experimental method. Any social structure or institution can be brought into question through the use of social intelligence guided by universalizing ideals, leading to reconstructive activity which enlarges and reintegrates the situation and the selves involved, providing at once a greater degree of authentic self-expression and a greater degree of social participation. (p. 384)

The authentic organization will always involve shared values and goals. The ultimate goal is that of promoting the growth or development of both individual participation and the collective outcomes envisioned. Given this view, differences are not to be erased but rather liberating possibilities for new reconstructions are made possible through interactions of creative individuals with interest groups.

Although Putnam and Putnam (1993) emphasized the importance of the social as well as the dynamics of multiple groups in forging a pluralistic democracy, Rosenthal (1986) stressed the interactions of creative leaders and the communities of interest in reframing institutions. Education is central. We need to recognize the importance of the school as the form of life needed for the redesign of schooling itself. The new school should also teach for the new form of pluralistic social order. It is vital to see democracy and school reform as requiring individual selves as well as groups. Their interests (whether ethnic, racial, religious, or gender) form the points of conflict and consensus by which the new school order will develop.

We must take the plural interests of Americans seriously but must not encourage a politics of difference that substitutes narrow self-interest for national identity. We must see critical pragmatism as a philosophy that treasures a distinctly American hope. A quick survey of schools in the United States reveals a serious erosion of pride and confidence in our nation. Although individual and plural voices are important, the harmony of a cultural democracy pluralism is not to be denied.

Conclusions

Any proposal to reform schools must take seriously the underlying values of the democratic nation in which such schools are located. The criterion for choosing the arrangement of school life resides in the values of democracy, values that make it possible for choices to be defended. What are these democratic values? We have identified these as (a) a dedicated belief in the worth of the individual and the importance of the individual in participation and discussion regarding school life; (b) a belief in freedom, intelligence, and inquiry; (c) a conviction that projected designs, plans, and solutions be results of individuals pooling their intelligent efforts within communities.

Democracy may become the standard for choosing the good school arrangement because it is the standard for choosing the good life. These democratic values are ideals, and any democratic people may fall short of realizing them completely. These criteria for assessing what is good, in this case what is good in the way of school organization, are located in the developing experiences of the community. As Gould (1988) wrote: "Democracy is more than a mere means for the achievement of basic values. Rather, it is the best and proper institutional embodiment that gives expression to the values of life and of equal positive freedom" (p. 281). Democracy provides for decision making that is an expression of freedom as well as ethical declarations of profound importance. It is the failure to see this dual role of judgment in democratically organized school communities that hampers efforts to introduce both the democratic and the critical pragmatic into discussions of a new school order.

In the foregoing I have argued that the method of critical pragmatic intelligence may be found in the efforts of the great social philosophers of the past as well as the current writings of theoreticians of a speculative turn to deal with both the problem of organization and democracy in a changing world. The notion of democracy must be taken seriously if social arrangements in school spaces are to prosper and be fruitful in the future. It is painfully obvious that new forms of community life are on the horizon; however, they cannot be realized unless they draw on the self-same elements of local community life already available to us. Chaos approaches threaten democratic plans for school reform. We must be on the alert to reject skeptical postmodern cosmologies and be ready to embrace affirmative postmodernism that prizes discursive and participatory democracy for schools.

4

𝔞

Three Efforts to
Restructure Schools

On the Receiving End of Structure

Joseph A. Fernandez (1993), former chancellor of the New York
public school system, put it this way in speaking of his leadership
style while pushing through school restructuring reforms in Miami
and New York City:

> My stance as a manager has always been this simple: there'll
> be no surprises. I demand the same of my staff. If I'm
> dealing with the board, I do my homework, base my case
> on the best information I have and present it. And if any-
> body makes a better case, and I want to modify mine, I say
> so. But when I've reached a position (or made a decision), I
> stick with it. People appreciate that. (p. 170)

The story of school restructuring in recent years is the tale of
modernist managerial philosophy running headlong into postmodern cultural changes. The narrative has been one of exportation of

75

modified structure, typically from the top down, against a cultural background of New Age chaos and irrationality. In cities large and small, school reform has been perceived by administrators, teachers, and parents as just another program to be implemented. The mindset of modern school keeping rests undisturbed. Where grassroots movements, which challenge the rational and technical views of education, move to redesign schools they are necessarily messy and difficult to monitor and assess. Many career administrators shy away from schooling changes they cannot rationally control.

Research so affected our modern conception of school organization that reformers accepted unquestioningly the tools and conceptual frameworks from noneducational disciplines. As a result, writings about schools are laced with social, structural, and functional terms and theories. Schools are assumed to be rational, structural entities that operate according to their own rules. The match between schools and business/industry is taken for granted. The result is that the people living and learning within the school are regarded as determined by the organization. It follows that reform is reduced to restructuring, reorganizing, or reconfiguring the organization. Those individuals who live and work within the institution of the school deal on a daily basis with structure. The schoolhouse is configured in precise ways, features of which differ from every other institution. We are taught first as students within the school and later as parents or members of schools that organization is a generic phenomenon and that the literature of business school professors may be translated unambiguously from factory to schoolhouse. Nothing could be further from the truth.

The present crisis in education is a crisis of definitional boundaries of schooling that threatens the very existence of public education in the United States. What counts as the organization of the school is a disabled institution produced by cultural and social forces outside the doors of the school. Interests are largely dictated by social scientists and bureaucrats who have defined the organization and continue to tinker with that design in the name of restructuring. Add to this the pressure from the public to make schools solve the exact social problems that disable it internally, and you have a very real "imperfect panacea" (Perkinson, 1991). The schools no doubt will continue to be called on to solve the social problems of the age, no matter what these may be.

Efforts to restructure schools thus are hobbled by the fact that few practitioners within the institution of the school can see their way clearly enough to discern viable new modes of association to be adopted. Experts are largely embedded in rationalist, positivist, and behavioral mind-sets. Educators are blindsided by their peculiar positioning within the organizational site. Hess (1991) has pointed out that few innovative ideas regarding reorganization emerge from within the ranks of school people. Most leaders are flamboyant outsiders or caretaker insiders. According to Archbald (1993), what is interesting is the "widespread unwillingness or inability to conceive of structurally different educational alternatives" (p. 385). This lack of imagination results in the breakdown of school reform efforts even before they begin.

Needed in today's school reforms is a commitment to the philosophic and moral responsibility to deal with issues and to see across the boundaries separating today's school organization from the larger culture. Proposals for school reform typically include emphasis on student achievement, a decentralized authority structure, emphasis on community, teacher and staff development, and a results-driven accountability (Archbald, 1993). Each of these elements may be treated well or poorly by restructuralists.

The following pages will analyze examples of restructuring at the state, district, and local levels. It is typically argued that school reform of an organizational type cannot take place unless someone or some group gives up some of its power and control. Neither teachers nor principals can restructure their work unless central authority allows it. This philosophy of school change is inherently defeatist and delays the true tale of school redesign. Subsequent pages will show how school organizing is a continuous process that reveals neither chaos nor complete rational order. Although school restructuring is taken as top-down, school reconstruction and design must be seen as aesthetic-moral and democratic in nature.

Historical Efforts to
Restructure Schools in the United States

The school restructuring movement currently sweeping advanced democratic nations such as the United States and Australia is not the first such reform movement to seek to reorganize schools (Tyack, 1990). In the first half of the 19th century, the common school reform movement under the leadership of Horace Mann and Henry Barnard pushed for the centralization of control over schools and the creation of a uniform curriculum and teaching methods. After World War I, the United States experienced the progressive education reform movement. This reform had as its goal the realignment of the power basis of schooling as well as the reshaping of educational goals.

The extent to which the common school reform movement of the first half of the 19th century and the progressive education movement of the first half of the 20th were cohesive and consistent efforts to reform American education along agreed-on lines is debatable. Michael Katz (1968) challenged the singular belief in common schools, and John Childs (1956) argued that the divisions that separated the various wings of progressive education should not be seen as insurmountable. However, hindsight reveals that the cleavages in these reforms eventually stifled the public schools (Cremin, 1961). The following overview shows how the historical record of these large-scale efforts to restructure American schools can be instructive.

Early failures of school restructuring. By most accounts the common school reform movement resulted in a centralization of schools, uniformity of curriculum and teaching methods, standardization of assessment and promotion procedures, introduction of teacher-training normal schools, and so forth. The progressive movement, in its school restructuring dimension, resulted in scientifically managed institutions that were calibrated with precision.

The common school's legacy was the state school bureaucracy and a conception of the educational leader as business and industry magnate. Business techniques influenced the preparation of school administrators. This model for school leadership resulted in a new type of superintendent and principal who served as caretakers, micromanaging the educational operation with an eye to financial costs.

To understand school reform today, we must view efforts arising out of multiple springs of discontent.

The 1960s. The "open classroom" idea was taken from the British infant schools and grafted on the public schools in the United States. New schools were built without the typical modular classroom interior landscape. Older schools were remodeled along more open floor plans. Unfortunately, teachers were not adequately prepared to teach in the open classroom, the open spaces were noisy and distracted children from learning, and parents came to react critically to the perceived disorder that the open classrooms brought to their children's lives.

The 1970s. Jencks (1972, 1979) argued that schools really were not making a difference for America's working population. Inequalities existed in the distribution of wealth, and schools had no impact on this fact. Carnoy and Levin (1976) echoed Jencks and argued that educational reform was seriously limited by gross social problems that were produced by the basic nature of our economic, political, and social system. A society resting on inequalities in power positions, income, and social status was not capable of changing those relations through schools. In addition, social problems such as racism, unemployment, poverty, and sexism could be altered only by changing the sociopolitical and economic structure from competitive and profit driven to an arrangement of equal and cooperative living. The bottom line was that schools reflect life; they never change it.

In the 1970s social scientists seemed to abandon the possibility of using the schools to reform American society. American education came under federal and state pressures because of a new interest in equality, freedom, and human rights. The antiwar feeling, Black separatism, and other movements punctuated the American interest in individual choice. It was not surprising to see the schools influenced by this shift in thinking (Ravitch, 1983).

Fantini (1976) first highlighted the logic of choice in the selection of public schools. He argued that parents had the right to pick the best public institution for their children. Soon the courts were filled with litigants challenging the unitary school systems of the United

States to respond to their needs. African Americans, disabled persons, women, and other groups petitioned the courts for redress and corrections. Americans became increasingly disenchanted with their public schools.

The 1980s. Three forces met to push for school restructuring during this decade: (a) Stimulated by *A Nation at Risk* (National Commission on Excellence in Education, 1983), a series of reports, studies, and sponsored research criticized public education; (b) sloganeering efforts such as "excellence in education" prompted a reexamination of schools; and (c) the Republican political philosophy represented by President Ronald Reagan and Secretary of Education William J. Bennett gained national attention in its criticism of public education. American public schools were compared with Japanese institutions and found to be seriously underserving students. It was argued that competition with Japan required school reform to provide better educated workers. "Educational excellence" became the battle cry. Per-pupil expenses were too high, pupils were dropping out, and those who graduated were poorly prepared for work or college. The list of ills sounded familiar. A conservative backlash much like that which felled the progressive education movement in the 1950s reverberated throughout the nation. Hence it was not surprising when *school restructuring* appeared in the school reform literature. The public had been convinced by scholars, journalists, and various interest groups that the "one best system" no longer delivered the goods. What was required, the reformers in the 1970s and 1980s stressed, was a reorganization of public education (Cibulka, 1975; Oakes, 1985).

Today. Contemporary attitudes toward educational reform in the United States grew from the turbulent decades of the 1970s and 1980s. Reformers are forming coalitions with surprising recommendations for school reorganization. There were two waves of reform in the 1980s. The first wave centered on *accountability*. Schools were to be reformed against measures of economic efficiency. This phase was launched by the National Commission on Excellence in Education's (1983) report, *A Nation at Risk: The Imperative for Education Reform*. This document stressed that U.S. schools were mediocre and in need of change. The report was followed by a number of similar publications seeking to make schools more accountable to the public. "Higher standards" was the clarion call. Teachers were severely criticized for lackluster performance, higher graduation standards were advocated, and comparative checks of schools and districts were to be fashioned.

The second modernist wave of reform in the mid-1980s targeted school organization and structure, teaching, and parent-school relationships. The demand here was for *restructuring*. Reformers reasoned that merely setting higher standards was insufficient; the institution of the school itself needed changing (Hess, 1991). Attached to such redesign were several key component changes: parent choice, teacher empowerment, decentralization, and site-based management.

Representatives from the political left, right, and center found themselves now viewing school reform through the lens of restructuring. Some groups formed strange alliances. For example, members of the Far Right and the Far Left political persuasions advocated complete elimination of organized public schooling as we know it via school vouchers. African Americans on the left joined with conservative Whites on the right in advocating separate, single-race schools. On the Far Left, critical pedagogues saw schools as worth preserving but undemocratic and repressive. Members of this group wished wholesale school redesign to incorporate greater democratic participation. More moderate communitarians supported this idea of greater democratization.

Two educational research thrusts informed school restructuring: effective schools and participative management (Hess, 1991). Although effective teaching researchers had hit fallow ground, new life was given to the concept of effectiveness when it was moved to measuring entire schools. Studies were spun out that sought to link individual schools to transnational norms of effectiveness.

Participative management came from business and industry, where companies such as Chrysler had successfully restructured work operations by placing more decision making on the assembly line. The factory metaphor had always been welcomed by school administrators, thus the transfer of such decision making to local schools from the central office seemed logical. What was good for business was good for the schools!

The upshot was that the literature on school restructuring reform was laced with proposals to redesign schools, but attached to these were social and political agendas that differed dramatically in their assumptions regarding who could speak for the schools, who had the solutions to school failure, and who would be in charge. Key reform elements such as decentralization of education, building local school communities, staff development, empowerment of teachers and parents, and emphasis on accountability and results popped up in widely differing political philosophies (Archbald, 1993).

The American penchant for using common sense and getting the task done has largely voided discussion regarding the deeper philosophical ideas driving reform. Practical redesigners deal most concretely with the many details of redesign. Many of these reformers provide handbooks, guidebooks, and manuals for educators to follow in developing redesigns. Those educational writers interested in the deeper layers of schooling, such as Elmore (1990) and Murphy (1991), offer overviews of the phenomenon of school restructuring built on earlier modernist theories of role, function, and structure. It is significant to see that many of the writers dealing with school restructuring adopt views that reflect more a matter of tinkering with the existing structures to make them more viable. Although on the surface pragmatic, these views tend to be expedient and shortsighted, overlooking the shifts in American culture and philosophy that inform the initial reform call itself.

Three Levels of School Organizational Change

While keeping an eye on the biases of modernist theorizing that we all carry to a project of empirical investigation of school restructuring examples, it is possible to adopt the pyramidal configuration of school bureaucracy. This legacy of the historic views of school organization informs any attempt to locate and evaluate efforts to restructure based on the success-failure criteria of the movement itself. When we lay on the categories of decentralization, teacher empowerment, and parental choice, we may ask whether these norms have been matched in practice.

A second way to evaluate the school restructuring movement is to ask how well the reform mirrors postmodern visions of our changing American culture. To do this requires looking beyond mere structural fit and measuring school redesign against the conditions of postmodern culture. Of concern here is whether the examples of redesign represent democratic values of (a) worth and dignity of individuals, dialogue, and participation; (b) intelligence and inquiry; and (c) communal decision making.

Characteristics of contemporary school restructuring. What is loosely termed *restructuring* has occurred in all 50 states at the levels of individual schools, multischool districts, and entire state educational systems. Characteristically, restructuring involves reforming curriculum and instruction; shifting authorities and decision making closer to the schools; reconfiguring administrative, staff, and teaching roles and responsibilities; and introducing some type of measurement or assessment system to ensure efficiency. To some extent all of these features, in various amounts, develop in school restructuring efforts.

There is an implicit assumption that for the goals of reform to be achieved—whether they be greater equity of school effectiveness, school efficiency, student performance, teacher empowerment, or parental choice—the schools must be restructured. This fundamental belief seems to distinguish the present set of reforms from all prior efforts. There is a new embrace of the corporate and business experts' manifesto that what is wrong with organizations is the way they are organized and run. Increasingly following the philosophies of Tom Peters (*Liberation Management,* 1992) and other business administration gurus, school bureaucrats are accepting the view that individuals are creative and innovative workers and that this creativity and imagination can be managed only by adopting a laissez-faire policy. Implicit in all these reforms is the accepted notion that people are by their very nature good laborers and that the problems of low productivity and competition with Japan are the result of useless layers of middle managers who have insulated the people closest to the product from the corporate leadership. Increasing line workers' productivity, whether in the classroom or the corporate office, is seen as a function of hands-off leadership that inspires, encourages, and evokes the positive nature of superior labor.

Each of the examples of school restructuring may be characterized by answers to three questions: (a) *Who's talking?* How have choice and participation changed? How are the lines of communication set up, who is accountable for what, and who engages in discussion and participates and to what extent? (b) *Who knows the answer?* How much teacher empowerment is evident? Because teachers are central figures in instruction, what changes in teaching and learning are found? How have pupils and school life changed? (c) *Who's minding the store?* How evident are decentralization and site-based management in the new restructured organization scheme? How is the organization run, what type of arrangements are found, and who are the leaders?

State Restructuring: Kentucky

On April 11, 1990, Governor Wallace Wilkinson signed into law the Kentucky Educational Reform Act (see Kentucky Department of Education, 1990) and thus launched statewide restructuring of education. A Kentucky Supreme Court opinion (*Rose v. The Council for Better Education, Inc.,* 1989) prompted this reform by declaring unconstitutional the then-operative state system of education. Betty Steffy (1993a), in perhaps one of the most thorough treatments of state-mandated educational reforms (*The Kentucky Educational Reform: Lessons for America*), has provided a catalog of events and characters leading up to and implementing KERA.

Kentucky had a history of poor performance in schooling its children and youth; it was often ranked near the bottom in standard measures of elementary and high school completion. Financial expenditures for education in the state ranged from $80 per pupil in poorer districts to $3,716 in wealthy districts. State revenue per pupil ranged from a low of $1,750 to a high of $2,753. Teaching supplies costs ranged from $8 to $259. The total state and local revenue supporting the schools in 1989-1990 was $2,004,770,000 (Steffy & English, 1994).

Historically, the curriculum in Kentucky schools was textbook driven. School administration was traditional, although some school boards and local superintendents encouraged some participatory models. Local school boards were powerful agents that dictated superintendent selection.

In 1985 a group of 66 school districts, along with seven boards of education and some 22 public school students, formed the Council for Better Education, Inc. and filed a class action suit testing the equity of school funding in Kentucky. The judge found Kentucky's system of school financing inefficient and discriminatory (Steffy & English, 1994). The recommendation was that a new system for financing schools had to be developed by the Kentucky General Assembly.

The case was appealed to the Kentucky Supreme Court in June 1989. The opinion rendered found the financing as well as the state system of public education unconstitutional. The Kentucky Supreme Court ordered the General Assembly to create an efficient system that was substantially uniform throughout the state. The General Assembly responded by creating a Task Force on Education Reform in July 1989. This task force was divided into three subcommittees with consultants hired to aid them. Out of these deliberations came recommendations and, ultimately, House Bill 940, the Kentucky Educational Reform Act, which was made law on July 13, 1990 (Steffy & English, 1994).

KERA invoked a billion-dollar tax increase over 2 years, established a nongraded primary school for grades K-3, implemented site-based management teams that included teachers, created preschool programs for at-risk children, and prohibited teachers from participating in school board election campaigns (Willis, 1991). Full-scale restructuring of Kentucky's school system will be achieved by 1996.

Like so many restructuring movements, the model driving Kentucky is one of assessment. By 1996 all of the state's schools will have students measured against international achievement standards. In large measure, KERA assumes that students from widely different socioeconomic situations may be tested and compared. The results of such statistical comparisons will be yardsticks for measuring the efficiency of the educational delivery system. Steffy and English (1994) reported that by 1993 the management, finance, and curricular changes had begun in Kentucky.

Kentucky's restructuring can be analyzed from three perspectives, by asking the three previously discussed questions.

Who's Talking?

Choice. Ostensibly, parents and students are to be given more choices in schooling. It is not clear that such choosing is done for the right reasons, however. Local schools are to involve parents in decision making. Curriculum and programs are to be responsive to parents' interests and needs. It is still too early to discover whether or not choice is working.

Accountability. New standards were instituted, and KERA centered on a statewide performance assessment system to check reform progress. The assessment system involved portfolios, performance event assessment, and open-ended responses to problems. Four levels of student performance were introduced: novice, apprentice, proficient, and distinguished. The goal was for all students in each school to test at the top two levels; however, in 1992 only 10% of the students did so (Steffy & English, 1994). By 1996 all students are to be tested relative to the six state curricular goals.

Perhaps more important, school report cards were developed so that individual schools could be compared with a "school accountability index" to be generated. Every 2 years schools would be given new goals called *thresholds* to aim for in their drive for accountability. If a school failed to achieve its goals, it would be labeled "in crisis" and experts would be called in to manage it. Initially, students in grades 4, 8, and 12 were tested in the 1991-1992 school year, with some 90% of children failing to meet the standards (Steffy & English, 1994).

Overall, KERA has imposed a top-down reform of schooling in the state of Kentucky that rivals any reform since Horace Mann reconstructed Massachusetts's educational system in the first half of the 19th century.

Who Knows the Answer?

A series of programs has affected the managerial philosophy and has attempted to improve parent-school relationships. The preschool program, a new primary school for K-3, the Extended Services Program, and a program designed to join social services and education called Family Resource/Youth Service Centers were created. Independent evaluations of these programs found that where they were implemented they appeared to be working (Steffy & English, 1994).

KERA's programs, begun on a strong footing, seem to address the needs of parents who demand more from the schools. Researchers have reported that changes in the American family have yielded multiple crises in society. By assuming more responsibility for parenting in loco parentis, Kentucky's schools relieve some of the burden of child rearing from parents.

Who's Minding the Store?

As part of the reforms in Kentucky, the entire state educational system was reorganized. The state department of education was completely gutted. The Education Professional Standards Board (EPSB) was created to reorganize the Kentucky Department of Education. The elected position of state superintendent of education was abolished. An appointed commissioner of education post was created. New school councils were established. Local school boards lost the power to hire teachers and staff to the superintendent. School boards were targeted. Stiffer rules prevented the members from hiring relatives, removing superintendents at will, and in other ways ensuring their power against public control. Principals, too, had their power curtailed with new antinepotism laws.

Perhaps one of the most successful features of the reform in Kentucky was the increase in pay for teachers. During the first 2 years of KERA and as a result of the revised funding formula, teachers' salaries increased on average by 16%, moving Kentucky's teachers to 29th in the nation in pay (Steffy & English, 1994).

As Steffy and English (1994) reported, the most important change was the formation of the school councils to ensure student achievement. These councils were made up of three teachers, two parents, and the principal as chairperson. School councils were given fiscal, curricular, teaching, and managerial responsibility. It was anticipated that councils would encounter criticisms from the school boards. The Kentucky Supreme Court ruled that councils could not be abolished by the boards, thus ensuring one key part of the democratization process.

Finance. In school restructuring financial issues are central. The SEEK (Support Education Excellence in Kentucky) formula for financing education was implemented in 1989, and by 1992 support for schools had risen from about $1.2 billion to nearly $2.1 billion. Taxpayers had seen their contributions to education rise sharply.

Because school revenues were based on property taxes, the new financing scheme sought to achieve equality by supplementing property-poor school districts. Local school district revenues leaped between 1989-1990 and 1991-1992. It was not unusual for a property-poor district to have a 50% increase in funds. But even the wealthy districts saw an increase of from 10% to 18% during the same time period. As Steffy and English (1994) reported, the analysis of funding equity reveals that the formula works.

City Restructuring: Chicago

During the 1980s mounting pressure was put on the public school system of Chicago to change its ways. The *Chicago Tribune* newspaper, then Secretary of Education William Bennett, and various citizen groups hammered away at the behemoth public school system. The schools and superintendent came under fire for a variety of reasons. Fiscal mismanagement left the schools barely operative and evidenced disproportionate funding of noninstructional jobs. School dropout rates were escalating. Minority students were appearing in larger and larger numbers on the special education roles. The ranks of the administrators were thickening at an alarming rate. ACT scores were dropping precipitously, and graduation rates were off (Hess, 1991).

For these and other reasons, restructuring was offered as the solution to the ills besetting the public schools of Chicago. On October 11-12, 1989, voters put in place local school councils (LSCs) with some 5,420 members. The Chicago School Reform Act of 1989 (P.A. 84-126) sought to bring Chicago pupils up to national standards in achievement, attendance, and graduation. School restructuring in Chicago reallocated funds and gave local school councils power to select a school improvement plan and to do its own staffing (Hess, 1991).

Reform goals were specified, but two topped the list: (a) ensuring that all students achieved proficiency in reading, writing, math, and higher order thinking and (b) making sure that students attended school and graduated at rates comparable to national norms (Hess, 1991). The reform reallocated monies so that the administrative bureaucracy did not grow any further and funds were moved to the elementary and high schools.

Who's Talking?

Choice. Taking decision making from bureaucrats and relocating it in the hands of parents and community members have been the keystones of the Chicago school reform. The city is large, and local communities have suffered at the hands of downtown bureacracy. Financial resources have been disproportionately allocated to upper layers of school administration in the central office. Although not all communities have taken the initiative and accepted the charge of democratic localism, nearly one half of the schools appear to be actively engaged in some kind of local governance (Bryk, Easton, Kerbow, Rollow, & Sebring, 1994).

Accountability. Although testing is a key part of Kentucky's school reforms, Chicago had already tested and evaluated students enough to realize that they were failing by all standards. The Chicago School Reform Act established goals in reading, mathematics, and so forth to be accomplished within 5 years. The aim was to move the city's schools to seek to achieve national levels of excellence.

Realistically, the reformers realized that more was needed than higher test scores. If reallocation of money, the empowerment of teachers, and the successful implementation of school site-based management were achieved, then it was reasoned that improved student retention rates and learning would follow.

Who Knows the Answer?

The Chicago reforms assumed that the teacher would have to play a key role in improving the schools. Teachers were to be given a voice in the local school council. Rather than bashing teachers for their inadequacy and imposing "teacher-proof materials," as had been the case under previous superintendent Ruth Love, the new philosophy saw teachers as often the first professional in their family, dealing with parents who had considerably less education. Site-based decision making presumed that teachers, as they were, could take part in the governance of the school.

Envisioned was a local school in which teachers working collaboratively developed new teaching materials and techniques. Teachers were taught to move beyond the local model of "my classroom" to work collaboratively with others. Teachers were expected to be active leaders and planners of school reorganization and to have a major voice in curricular decisions, textbook selections, and the shaping of the instructional program of the school (Hess, 1991). This did not happen. In fact, the principal was deemed the instructional leader of the school, thus compromising the role of teachers in instruction, although teachers had the last say through their representation on the local school council, which played an active role in the evaluation of the principal.

Little was done to prepare teachers for their new role. Some universities offered courses for teachers—but too few and too little. As Hess (1991) concluded, largely missing in the effort to assist school-level professionals with the new skills they needed to make school restructuring work was a dedicated administration. Staff development programs that had been in place under the old regime continued virtually unchanged.

Who's Minding the Store?

Each school was required to have a local school council made up of parents, community representatives, teachers, and the principal. Subdistrict councils were also created for about 10 subdistricts. These councils had powers similar to the LSCs but coordinated the operations of the schools within areas. A board nominating commission was formed to provide nominations to the new Chicago School Board, now seen largely as a jurisdictional rather than as a managerial body (Hess, 1991).

Tangential to the reforms was a teacher empowerment effort. Chicago did not recognize the teachers to be as important as parents and community. Teachers were seen as linked to the principal via the Professional Personnel Advisory Committee (PPAC), which advised the principal and LSC on educational programs and the new school improvement plan. Teachers sat on the LSC but were outnumbered.

Principal power too was severely narrowed: The principal was seen as the instructional leader. Principals now were beholden to the LSC rather than administrative higher-ups. Principals were charged with personnel decisions, assessing (along with the LSC and PPAC) the gains of the reform plan. Some additional funds were given to the principal. Most problematic was the fact that the principal was accountable to his or her LSC and could be removed if deemed ineffective (Hess, 1991).

Simply put, the Chicago reform curtailed the efforts of the superintendent to build the central office at the expense of the districts. The legislation sought to move power and control from the center out to the parents and community representatives within school districts. Actually, this decentralization had been the norm in the early 20th century and had been attacked as inefficient then. Now the urban schools were recast into more locally democratic units that had been so cumbersome and unproductive in the first half of the century.

Finance. The Chicago restructuring effort sought to reallocate resources within the city school districts. The Chicago School Reform Act included two provisions that sought to change the disproportionality of funding. The first called for a cap to be placed on the costs of administering the system. This move was resisted by the general superintendent but ultimately resulted in a shifting of money from the central office to local schools. The typical elementary school received about $90,000 more in the first year, with the amount reaching $450,000 by the 4th year of implementation (Hess, 1991, pp. 107-109).

One area that continued to be testy involved the allocation of Chapter 1 funds. Although some of the money for Chapter 1 was shifted to local schools, much cash was retained by the central office for oversight costs. The Chicago management philosophy sought desperately to retain control over as much of its previous dynasty as possible.

Critics point out that the problems of school finance are far from over. Wide variance exists between wealthy school districts and property-poor districts. In the "Voice of the People" column of the *Chicago Tribune,* James T. Durkin (1993), faculty member at Morton College, reported that some of the school districts with the highest test scores were in the suburbs of the North Shore and northwest Cook County, as well as in the wealthiest areas of Du Page and Lake counties. In 1992, 29 north and northwest suburban Cook County districts averaged $6,939 in per-pupil expenditure, although the 37 south suburban districts averaged only $4,403. The recommendation: Impose equity funding throughout the counties of Illinois.

Still other critics point to the need to spread financial resources evenly across the state. Daume and Pardo (1993) noted that as the result of Chicago's school reforms, the city had to present a balanced budget before schools could open in the fall. Such a requirement was not visited on the other school districts of the state of Illinois. Some 111 school districts were in serious financial difficulty in the fall of 1993. These schools were underfunded, but the governor and legislature had failed to deal with this problem. It was proposed by Daume and Pardo of the League of Women Voters of Chicago that a fair and adequate income tax be instituted while reducing the property tax as the primary funding source for schools.

The financial mechanisms for supporting schools are far from agreed on, and it is clear that inequities exist between large city systems and suburban and rural districts. Equity continues to be a thorny problem for reformers.

In conclusion, Hess (1991) pointed out that the Chicago reform was a bold one and built on both research and the uniqueness of the city. Epps (1994) gave the Chicago restructuring reform a mixed report card. All schools have LSCs and have submitted school improvement plans. About 80% of the schools have made efforts to improve school and community relations and increase parent participation. But only one third of the schools are beginning to make progress, with another third making good progress. Critics have fastened on to a salient feature of the Chicago experiment: its democratic temper. Some argue that by giving the schools back to the people via democratic governance, the capacity of the professional educators to do their work is curtailed, and failure is ensured

(Chubb & Moe, 1990). Principals report that they wish they had greater control over their schools, particularly over teachers (Epps, 1994).

School District Restructuring: West Feliciana Parish, Louisiana

Nestled along the Mississippi River in rural Louisiana, the parish of West Feliciana is characterized as a tourist haven, with stately plantations and rolling acres of live oaks. Major income sources stem from the Entergy River Bend Nuclear Power Plant and a paper mill. The school district is the largest employer in the parish. Property taxes do not form the base for financing schools in Louisiana. The state revenues and local or parish money from oil and gas leases provide financial support. There is no great source of supplemental revenue from oil or gas in West Feliciana parish; however, the parish manages its resources well compared to other parishes in the state.

With a population of less than 15,000 (about 5,000 prisoners are held at Angola State Prison), West Feliciana Parish is a small rural parish about an hour's drive from Baton Rouge, the state capital. There are four schools in the parish: a prekindergarten-2nd grade school (with allied family services), a 2nd-6th grade school, a prekindergarten-6th grade school near the prison, and a single high school with grades 7-12.

The parish is 51% Black and 49% White. No private schools exist within the parish, although some parents send their children to a private school in Woodville, Mississippi. A beginning teacher in West Feliciana schools is paid $20,196 per school year. Even after 25 years of teaching, no teacher in Louisiana—even with a doctorate—can earn more than $31,000. Teachers in the state of Louisiana have not received a pay raise since 1988. Therefore, teaching, measured by salary levels, is not granted the professional status found in other employment fields.

First, it is important to point out that Louisiana, unlike Kentucky, has no experience with a legislative mandate for school restructure. The restructuring that has occurred has been at the district or school level. The Board of Elementary and Secondary Education (BESE), which governs the schools of the state, has shown no burning interest in restructuring to date. However, this is not to say that the legislature will not invoke some restructuring plan(s) of its own in the future.

One must understand the political climate of the state. Louisiana has been termed "a banana republic" because of its long history of centralized authority (Huey Long), corruption, and penchant for backward ways. Governed more like a Latin American country, Louisiana has had the wealth (oil and gas) in the past to pay for its inefficiencies. As the 21st century approaches, it is apparent that Louisiana will have to do something to bring its fiscal house in order. Greater democratization does not seem to be in the cards. Although efforts to reform teacher certification and retention flopped under the leadership of Governor Buddy Roemer, the current governor, Edwin Edwards, appears not to desire to become the last "education governor" touting school reform (Maxcy & Maxcy, 1992).

Thus when surveys were made of the state's school districts, it was with the understanding that whatever restructuring was going on did not have the teeth of any central mandates from the ruling bodies of Louisiana. It is therefore all the more momentous to find respondents indicating ongoing restructure. West Feliciana Parish schools showed a surprising number of restructuring efforts (Applied Technology Research Corporation, 1992).

Who's Talking?

Choice. Parents and students seem to have more opportunities to speak, but choice is still limited to a few schools and teachers. The parish is small and has few educational options for students and parents.

Accountability. New structures for accountability are in process in West Feliciana Parish schools. Teacher accountability has been a hot issue in the state for a number of years after a failed attempt at statewide teacher assessment. Principals decide on tenure cases, but few exercise their power to refuse poor teachers tenure.

A comprehensive assessment model for this parish's restructuring reforms has been created but has not been implemented. Assessment of West Feliciana reforms is the most problematic piece of the reform puzzle.

Who Knows the Answer?

Surveys of West Feliciana schools reveal an emphasis on introducing new programs and combining offerings. Programs for special needs students stress the inclusion of students with various disabilities into the regular classroom. Alternative programs are in place for non-college-bound students. The high school does not fully include special needs students, but progress is being made in this direction. Chapter 1 funds and monies from other sources are united to provide a combination remedy for educational problems.

Educational technology is being used in innovative ways. Teachers are assuming new roles for their teaching specialties. An early dismissal of students on Mondays allows teachers to plan and work collaboratively on curriculum and instruction. Students with special needs are receiving more help than under the previous organizational structure.

Who's Minding the Store?

West Feliciana Parish schools are undergoing governance restructuring. More parental involvement in school decisions is evidenced. Parents may be pleased with the greater number of social services connected with the schools. There is a large amount of school-business collaboration. Some site-based management is indicated but may well be a leadership characteristic of the principal.

Finance. Fiscal change is a part of West Feliciana's restructuring. Chapter 1 and special education monies have been fused and mingled. However, of all of the components of West Feliciana reform, finance is the least restructured. The funding formula remains state mandated with little flexibility available for equalization.

To understand this dimension of Louisiana's school restructuring efforts, one must understand the funding processes for public schools. As previously stated, property taxes are not (and never have been) central to financing schools. The state provides "minimum foundation" monies to each school district, and these are often supplemented by oil and tax revenues from the school itself. By these measures, West Feliciana is rural but not poor, having oil money and state support.

Critiques of School Restructuring

Liberal Modernist Assessments of Restructuring

In the foregoing analysis, I have examined the efforts of Kentucky, Chicago, and West Feliciana Parish to restructure by measuring these efforts using implicitly modernist standards. This tends to be an insider treatment of the restructuring movement. Critiques form curious conclusions. The modernist arguments seem to boil down to this: Because the reform is one of restructuring, we must test the structural features introduced relative to prior structure. Have new groups of persons, not traditionally central in school decisions, been heard from (parent empowerment)? Have instruction and curriculum been modified (teacher empowerment)? And is there evidence of changes in leadership (decentralization and site-based management)?

Modernists seek to identify the restructuring of productive work of the participants, administrators, teachers, and pupils. Then the organizational structure relative to its decentralization is analyzed. Last, the domain of teaching and learning is examined to test for increases in test scores and other measurable outcomes assumed to stem from reconfiguration (Murphy, 1991).

The difficulties with this modernist approach are fascinating to behold. The restructuring is compared with the past structure but with the assumption that shifts in control are always at a price. Roles are redefined, responsibilities reallocated, and outcomes laid open to doubt. There is a tendency to see new education settings and processes as shifts in responsibility, and the rational-technical mode of thought continues into the new structure. For example, although in the past the teacher was considered a worker, now the student is seen as the worker. The structuralist grid simply shifts to embrace new constituencies (Murphy, 1991). Responsibility for outcomes shifts from teachers as agents to the "core technology" or "delivery system" of instruction (pp. 50-71). Structuralist and technologist viewers of school restructuring lament a lack of focus on the core technology of teaching. Modernist bureaucracy assumes the need for direction and control of staff to ensure that the continuous high standards in organizational outcome are met. These processes of instruction are incapable of self-regulation. They suggest that teachers and instruction must be monitored, supervised, and evaluated by managers.

Murphy (1991) went so far as to say: "I believe . . . that revisions in organizational and governance structures should be more tightly linked to revisions in curriculum and instruction" (p. 74). By first reforming teachers and instructional methods, the restructuring can be "backward mapped" from the student to other parts of the school. Such a move places the heat on teachers and removes the pressure for change from administrators. As Murphy phrased it: "It is time to redirect the restructuring spotlight on the classroom and the processes and activities that unfold there" (p. 93). In addition, the movement to redesign schools can be more carefully controlled by the administrators if power is retained in the office and responsibility rededicated in the foxholes. In accordance with modernist-structuralist theory, greater emphasis is placed on the students as variables in school reform success. Despite the admission that the postmodern-postindustrial culture has issued the schools nontraditional students of color, the consequence is to make students the cause of restructuring failure.

Although school restructuring is still too young to provide sufficient material for judgment of success or failure, some studies have raised questions about its course. Webb, Bondy, and Rose (1994) conducted 800 interviews in six Florida restructured schools and found four dilemmas faced by restructuring. This research team looked at mission, unification of stakeholders, risk taking, and leadership. They concluded that these restructured schools were failing to achieve restructure (only one actually succeeded and that one was a middle school). In five out of the six, there seemed to be no mission, stakeholders were not united, few teachers were risking new strategies, and no decision could be made as to who led the school.

It is not difficult, given this reading, to lapse into structuralist recommendations in an effort to recover the schools from the abysses. "What we need is a strong principal who will unite the teachers, telling them the mission and holding them accountable for that mission!" But to argue this way is to reestablish the bureaucratic system of structured education. Needed is an invocation of postliberal, postmodern-poststructural norms such that the participants (parents, students, and teachers) have a say about what is taught and what is learned. A new view of community and leadership that liberates and redirects the school toward its goal of making artful lives is required.

A Postliberal, Postmodernist-Poststructuralist, and Critical Pragmatic Critique

School restructuring may also be evaluated by laying these reform movements against democratic values and critical pragmatic processes. For democratic institutions such as schools to prosper, they must represent the larger democratic form of living within the social space of the schools. Success of the school reforms can be judged by the degree to which elements of pragmatic democracy are evident. Let us examine school restructuring in Kentucky, Chicago, and West Feliciana Parish from a critical pragmatic perspective.

Worth and Dignity of Individuals

Did the old organization marginalize groups that would have desired to speak? Was the playing field level? Was there equality of participation in forming the new design?

Steffy (1993b) pointed out that Kentucky's KERA educational reforms have been top-down. Required for their full success are bottom-up reforms. Once the standards had been created and the infrastructure had been put in place, there was a need to change what took place in classrooms. Steffy rightly found teachers as the most responsible agents for change within the classroom. To prepare teachers for implementing KERA, in-service instruction in such matters as performance assessment, site-based decision making, and teaching students of differing cultural backgrounds have been initiated. Teachers were to be provided 26 days devoted to professional development during the period 1990-1994. Eight regional service centers have been created to provide professional support and development. Steffy (1993b) wrote:

> More than tinkering with the present textbook-driven cur-
> riculum will be required. Creative, risk-taking educators
> will need to develop strong parental support, motivate and
> inspire dysfunctional families and children, and empower
> children to reach the intellectual and interpersonal stan-
> dards they are capable of achieving. If bottom-up restructuring
> is possible, the dedicated professional teachers in Kentucky
> will prove it can be done. (p. 44)

Steffy and Hess hit on a key insight: Risk-taking teachers will
need help, and the professionalism of teachers is critical for their
success in reform. Hess (1991) cataloged the facts of the case for
Chicago: Teachers were not properly instructed for their new roles
in the site-based managed schools of the city. Steffy's and Hess's
concerns regarding teachers and their need to be reeducated regarding reformist participation and discussion are on target.

In addition, although modernist restructuralists seek to introduce
professionalism as a corrective to school ineffectiveness, Hess (1991),
as an insider in Chicago school reform, noted that it was insufficient
to bring off school reform in that city. Bureaucratic growth was too
strong to be countered by educator professional norms being en-
forced. Thus even modernist assessments of school restructure see
the vacuous nature of technical controls over teachers.

A *New York Times* article titled "Teachers Feel Left Out of Reform"
(1993) stated that some 60% of teachers surveyed reported they had
yet to see any changes in their schools as the result of current
educational reforms. However, in schools in which major changes
had taken place, teachers felt better about their careers, schools, and
their ability to influence students' lives.

One goal of school restructuring has been the empowerment of
teachers. Taylor and Teddlie (1992) found little carryover in this
professionalism to caring for clients (students). Enhancing teachers'
work with students seemed not to emerge in the restructuring of
schools. In part this may be because teachers are still held accountable for student achievements measured by test scores. Restructured
schools then are being assessed using older style instruments that
teachers know how to teach for in the classroom. It seems little

wonder that the substance of restructuring in the classroom is so minimal.

Snauwaert (1993) pointed up another difficulty with teachers' participation in restructuring. Conflict results when teachers are encouraged to become more professional and community members are empowered. Restructuring finds these two groups vying over control of educational decision making. Local school councils and other site-based management units seem unable to address this problem. Snauwaert's solution is a constitutional democracy that emphasizes shared decision making among groups—a type of federal system for the schools. What he fails to see is that by giving free rein to parents and citizens, as well as professional educators, he has not concomitantly alerted everyone to a prior commitment to the norms of a democratic way of life. The moral-ethical requirement that choices be made that enhance the interests of participants (and here children must be included) as well as maximize the democratic values that make the whole process ongoing is slighted.

Empowerment. Giving inquiry back to the teachers is significant for the empowerment of educators. The teacher as researcher is one model that has been advocated. By allowing teachers to conduct research studies in their own schools, educators may be empowered through the understanding they acquire. Research into the practical problems educators face is professionally enabling as well.

Empowerment in democratic culture requires informed participants, and this means educators must be engaged in the processes of inquiry. Problem finding here is superior to problem setting (by elites). Inquiry authorizes empowerment, and leadership becomes the transaction of practical action. Educational redesign requires that educators engage in an empowering discourse-practice. Here critical pragmatism is needed.

Michel Foucault (1980) demonstrated that power is not something that can be acquired, seized, or shared. Rather, power is a relational concept known through its consequences. It is something over which we have very little control. Power is to be contrasted with authority, which is something we exert on others. Power relations are found embedded in all types of relations (sexual, pedagogical, familial, religious, etc.). Power relations are by their very nature unbalanced. Without cause power becomes evident only at points of disequilibrium (see also Sheridan, 1980).

Ira Shor (1992) pointed out that one aspect of empowerment is desocialization. We must come to unlearn received values, habits, and attitudes. We accept the organization of the school as it has been taught to us. We accept the norms and practices of the culture we inhabit because we are on the receiving end of acculturation. When educators introduce dialogue and debate regarding the existing socializing norms, a true transformation of an organization may occur. But if the socializing standards remain as they were, the school reorganization is a mere realignment of power and force vectored from new directions. The unempowered remain so.

Too often empowerment of teachers is given lip service, although the real power relations remain attached to authority structures and the desire to make teachers accountable for even more than before. Responsibility continues to operate structurally, with the classroom teacher taking on more tasks with less control. In state, city, and school district restructuring, this desire to move responsibility to those least powerful was profoundly evident.

The experiences of schooling become a focal point in which the meanings of human life are deconstructed and reconstituted over time. We are concerned here to test for the degree to which resistance to controlling power formed and reformed in the three contexts of state, city, and local school districts. The reading reveals teachers were insufficiently empowered to make restructuring work. There is little evidence of continuous resistance or transactional power-empowerment in the schools. Control over transactional phases of restructuring remains largely dominated by the same power groups.

A concrete example of where school redesign failed is the New York City schools. Former Chancellor Fernandez (1993) pointed out correctly that there must be a good relationship between superintendent and school board. By this he meant the board makes policy and the chief school officer implements it. However, when school boards begin to move across the boundary between policy maker and administrator, the relationship breaks down. School boards should not micromanage the schools, Fernandez argued. It is this perception of role that seems to result in superintendents of schools' tenure in office being on average about 3 years in duration. Sooner or later the board moves into management.

Fernandez neglected the other half of the danger: superintendents who become policy makers. This is an equally dangerous crossover seizure of role, taking away the policy-generation task of the school board. Superintendents have lost their posts on this score as well.

The pragmatic solution to this dilemma is one of focusing on the practical task at hand and the removal of role self-consciousness from the equation of school change. Roles need to flex in their definitions and boundary behaviors so that the successful achievement of goals is forthcoming. By locking up human actors in bureaucratic roles, the school reform effort is doomed almost from the start. Lessons from industry illustrate the point here: Where someone is yelling, "I'm the boss!," few cooperate and few wish to buy into the boss's vision. Authority gets in the way of creative action.

Democratic participatory leadership must be a part of the formation of the controlling aims, methods, and materials of the schools. These means ought to placed in the hands of teachers or their democratically chosen representatives.

Intelligence

To what degree were the constituents of these schools engaged in intelligent judgments? Did participants have full access to information? Did they have the resources to make good decisions?

At the root of it all, contemporary restructuring efforts are embedded in an early 20th-century philosophy of modernist liberalism. Restructurers believe rational management of educational structures will result in effective and efficient changes in student learnings. Technical manipulation of rules, roles, and responsibilities is supposed to yield highly effective outcomes in terms of pupil test scores. Attached to this rational-technical explanation of the nature and processes of schooling is the belief that such rigid configurations (a) can be changed and (b) ought to be changed. We are led to accept the logical step from social scientific description to policy recommendations. The value assumptions that are perpendicular to this linear intellectual movement from fact to recommendation are never surfaced. Yet without attending to questions of value, we are merely reinventing the wheel. The primary question for any restructure is: What is worthwhile?

In previous chapters, the importance of intelligence for critical pragmatism as well as postliberal democracy has been stressed. Without critical judgment exercised by all participants in the school—students, parents, teachers, and administrators—the effort to redesign schools will falter. It must be kept in mind that intelligence is promoted by aesthetic interests first. Qualities are had and then converted through thinking about them in terms of ends-in-view with critical attention to their workability and good-making characteristics. We have neglected to help participants in school restructuring recognize these features of intelligence and learn to use them in thinking of the objectives they set forth as missions and plans.

Community

The modernist belief understands the ends of the educational system as operationally specified, with attention focused solely on means. The moral, ethical, and other valuative matters are submerged or in other ways neglected. Reform becomes merely a regeneration or resuscitation of all the evils attached to the present system. There is little accomplished by curricular flattening of the bureaucracy if the educational system remains intact. As Steffy and English (1994) have reported, there is very low reliability attached to the performance assessment system adopted by states such as Vermont and Kentucky. It is that system and the managerial beliefs surrounding its invention and sustenance that need reform: Merely reconfiguring or realigning the old pieces of the structure and holding it accountable will not accomplish needed change.

On the correct side of the issue of professionalism (teacher professionalism being talked of most frequently) is the principal and the principalship. Restructuring plans seem to build on the authority of the principal in bringing about changes at the local school level. Yet experts on principal-preparation programs at the university level are keenly aware of the failures of such academic offerings in the face of a declining regard for principal authority (Quantz & McCabe, 1991). Only by moving away from a rhetoric that attempts to explain how programs train administrators to be more effective and efficient managers who will control organizations and by moving toward programs that educate people for shared democratic leadership shall the new school reforms begin to work. Creative and reflective persons are needed, and older notions of management and supervision are breaking down in the face of these new needs.

A further point needs addressing here. Although principal training programs in universities refer to "the principalship," there is no talk of "the teachership" or "the pupilship." Principals are elevated to a professional caste, and their characteristic difficulties are placed first. The aim is to maintain principal role, improve principal relationships, and show principals-to-be how to massage the rules of the organization for the benefit of their missions and imaginations. Until this focus is reconstructed and we remove the equivalency of principalship with leadership, the new school order will never arrive.

It may be further maintained that this wholesale reform is accomplished only where a shift in philosophy is undertaken. My argument is that only by focusing on the underlying sociopolitical way of life, in this case democracy, and on the needs of a postmodern 21st-century culture can we truly reform the social space of the school. The first step toward this larger scale reform is to change our way of thinking.

In the final analysis, however, the sacred elements of culture are difficult to change. School organization as we know it has been around since the 1830s. Resistance to planned change, no matter how beneficial the new plan is perceived to be, is more likely than not (Corbett, Dickson, Firestone, & Rossman, 1987).

The difficulty with the school restructuring plans in Chicago, Kentucky, and West Feliciana was that they failed to critically evaluate the research philosophies driving their reforms. The vocabularies and theoretical assumptions—modernist and structuralist—warranted and backed school restructuring with the consequence that these reforms are failing.

Leading the Organization of the School

Affixed to plans for school reorganization and redesign are new ideas about educational leadership. Change the organizational framework, and the leader must change as well. Contemporary postmodern theorists of education are calling for new notions of school leading, while cautiously listening to modernist demands for greater educational professionalism.

Educational leadership has never had a single definition, nor does it attach itself neatly and unambiguously to social arrangements such as schools. Schools have both developmental and egalitarian purposes. Leadership sets a particular problem for free democratic societies. Unlike totalitarian regimes in which citizens have no say as to who their leaders shall be, democracies require good leadership to grow from public selection processes. Our American republic was established, giving citizens the right to choose their leaders; thus the nature of that leadership became focal. However, although a democracy allows us to pick our political leaders on the basis of criteria (campaign promises, political platforms, voting records, experience, moral character, and decision-making ability—all play a role in our choices), our freedom to choose has not always resulted in the best type of leadership. There is another factor that must be included in the leadership-social-cultural way of life for the equation to work: a method of choosing.

For school reform to succeed in the postmodern era, attention must be paid to the types of communication, intelligence, and community required. The new school order must move from a management community to a community of sharing decision makers. A new type of leadership is needed, one that fuses sensitivity to beautiful ways of living with collaborative decision making.

New Ways to Think About Leadership in Schools

Aesthetic Leadership

Modernist authorities have come to stress the artful nature of leadership as a set of public and creative acts of leaders (Duke, 1986).

Leaders are individuals who engage in routine tasks and managerial duties, private in nature, and artistic public acts that gain attention of others by capturing the groups' imagination. How this attention getting operates is central to the aesthetics of leadership.

Duke (1986) sees aesthetic leaders doing three types of things: acting (dramatic in nature), designing, and orchestrating. However, in his conception of aesthetic leadership as well as the components of this notion, Duke continues to post the dichotomy of leader and followers, privileging the voice of the individual in charge. It is assumed that leading is a staged set of events, in which the role of the leader is mainly one of words.

Postmodern culture dictates that we adopt a different view of artistry. The aesthetic component of leading sees leading as a trans-actional set of experiences lending form to quality. Aesthetic leading in schools is the design of and experimentation with new forms of educative culture. A fuller interest in the composing of lives and the orchestration of experiences is stressed. Artful and creative, leading is committed to making qualitatively better lives for children and youth (Maxcy, 1991).

When we link this aspect of leadership to the natural capacity to create, through design, we have a vested commitment to a type of school space that is both continuous and emancipatory. Art becomes more general, as Dewey (1938) argued, when we find aesthetic quality within ordinary practices. Using the lens of the artist allows us to see the landscape of the school as a canvas to be worked. The life of the school as an arrangement takes on the character of an aesthetic work of art, and the classroom emulates the artist's studio. Composition and expression go together to form new and more beautiful teaching-learning settings.

Postmodern aesthetics (Jameson, 1991) are helpful here because the artist is engaged in both an analysis (deconstruction) and a reconstruc-tion of theme and medium. This may well aid school reform. Schools are said to be in chaos, too large and impersonal as organizations to help children very much. Critical pragmatic aesthetics allow us to attend to such complexity while proposing alterative configurations that are at once more pleasing and more unified.

Orchestrating the characters and materials of experience has overshadowed the richer deciphering and composing necessary to articulate an artistic outcome. We must keep in mind the delicate touch and sense of proportion, color, and shape that distinguish the artistry of leading. Postmodern culture has provided rich characterizations of such features of art in architecture, painting, and sculpture. Modernist critique is insufficient to reveal the meanings these forms may have for the future of our institutions.

A conception of pragmatic postmodern leadership necessary for the next generation of school redesigning entails a number of lessons drawn from the experiments in school restructuring to date. Consideration must be given to the steps that enable such leadership as it deals with the sociocultural chaos-order. An emancipated vision of leadership has a bearing on the crucial sociocultural issues facing the educator today. Issues such as discipline, drugs, and AIDS are all open to the methods of this reconceptualized leadership. Where human intelligence becomes a melioristic agency for an ongoing reconstruction of experience because of such problems, future experiences may be reordered to maximize human goods.

Certainly it is important to reconceptualize schools. The school is not simply an organizational complex, with a structure and function, peopled by workers exercising some role. A new interest has emerged in the ends toward which institutions and the people within them are pledged. By reconstituting human freedom through a new discursive democratic community and a new artistic and social pragmatism in the face of technology and totalitarianism, theorists are prompting a nonfoundational continuous conversation with concomitant edification (Bernstein, 1983; Campbell, 1992). As Bernstein pointed out, a new vision of people living and working in a nonobjectivist, nonrelativist world of local communities dedicated to praxis and phronesis has become possible—a world in which the process values of dialogue, conversation, ethical knowledge, practical discourse, and judgment are linked to the universal values of solidarity, participation, unity, and mutual recognition. It is important that this position is in sharp contrast to the restructuring reforms to date.

Aesthetic leadership must become democratic in nature. The democratic ethos calls for a full and free flow of information and for the open discussion of issues. To be democratic given this meaning of democracy as moral-ethical differs from mere exercise of expert techniques. Rather than being trained in particular narrow disciplines, educational leadership in school redesign must be moved to teachers, parents, and students.

The problems of education are capable of being resolved by participants in the smaller, autonomous schools but not in the present educational systems dominating the landscape today. Carefully formulated sets of guidelines are gathered from a variety of sources. A person's practical judgment is rather like his or her character or personality.

Leadership is so intimately tied to organization that we cannot think of one without the other. Leadership is so amorphous a concept that it becomes problematic how any reorganization of schools in the United States may draw on it systematically. Leading is too often reduced to mere administration and management. Seeing it in any other way is short-circuited by organizational barriers. Much work needs to be done to more fully analyze educational leadership as a particular type of leading as well as the distinct ways in which leadership becomes dispersed within schools.

A conception of leadership that at once sees leading as serving, exemplifying the moral-ethical character, and revealing an aesthetic capacity for creative design is needed. Only when management and administration in education are transformed into educational leadership of a transactional empowering type will plans for our next century's schools become truly postmodern. By focusing on practical judgment and decision making, laced with moral-ethical-religious-aesthetic value concerns, it is possible to relocate leadership in the site of the new school. But without a new notion of leadership, collaborative and communal in nature, it is difficult to see the new school restructuring succeeding. School reconstruction entails bottom-up initiatives that imply the type of participatory leadership outlined here.

The image of leadership involves reflective and practical group decision making in orchestrating complicated arrangements such as schools. By moving the focus away from leading as found in corporate management to the realm of the normative requirements of sociocultural institutions, we come up with an issues-driven model of school reordering. Here leading and ethics, leading and goal setting, and leading and development take on new meanings. Leaders neither are to take on a subservient role, working in the background engaging in "underlaborer" tasks, nor are they to become "philosopher-kings," privileged with nobility of station and knowledge.

Old-style modernist leadership, with its concern for ritual and performance, fails to see so much of human interaction as transacting leadership for the good of the group. By moving informal postmodern leading into the spotlight of formal organizational structures and by democratizing leadership by deauthorizing it and empowering self-initiating interpersonal structuring, we generate a type of problem-solving team leadership that will make a difference both in how schools look and in how they behave. A reconceptualization of leadership goes hand in glove with a reconstruction of the institution of the school.

Conclusions

We have seen how school restructuring at the state, city, and local levels is failing. The narrative of school restructure is one of formal realignments of money and control in various degrees of intensity. To date the school restructuring movement in the United States has been a modernist rationalization of the managerial mind. The goals are always the same: to save money, remove the blocks to efficient and effective administration, and so forth.

Schools have not been successfully restructured in Kentucky, Chicago, or West Feliciana Parish. What they need is school reform. Priority must be given to relocating school reform to the bottom of the pyramid of educational governance. We cannot legislate virtue. Only by reconfiguring the school reforms along the lines of participant democratic decision making and a commitment to the moral, ethical, aesthetic school and education can we achieve school reconstruction that will work for the postmodern age.

5

🖎

Cultural Diversity, Democracy, and Reconstructed Schools

Diversity and School Reform

The history of American education has been the story of the effort of public schools to control the lives of children in the name of "*the educational aim*." There has been a succession of aims and types of organization available to school leaders. Each period found educators espousing a different reason for incarcerating children and youth for a period of from 6 to 12 years.

The Early School Reform Era

In the early 1800s the Massachusetts legislature enacted public school laws that set up a free, tax-supported set of elementary schools. Under the lead of Horace Mann, secretary to the Board of Education, the system of schooling eventually included secondary schools and teacher-training institutions called normal schools. The vision of a perfectly articulated system of schools within which teachers would instruct children in basic subjects was so lockstep in nature that it was referred to as the Prussianization of the schools.

Although on the surface the schools were aimed at teaching children to be good scholars and citizens, the more subtle aims were to Americanize the immigrants and teach traditional values. Diversity was seen as the enemy. For those who controlled schooling—White Protestant males—the Irish-Catholic immigrants posed a threat. Mann's law office had been witness to a riot of dissident laborers. The reformers of American public schools adopted a uniform (albeit hidden) policy that pressed the newcomers into an "Anglo-Saxon conformity" (Katz, 1968).

Certainly the common school reform movement of Horace Mann set in place the organizational space called public school and invested this landscape with a manifest destiny of cultural conformity. Mann and his followers were obsessed with transforming immigrants into proper Bostonians. As a consequence, non-White, non-Protestant, non-Anglo-Saxon types suffered a future of either sociocultural marginalization or assimilation.

Ellwood Patterson Cubberley

Stanford University professor and "father of school administration" Ellwood Patterson Cubberley taught school administrators in the first decades of the 20th century. He believed that the only way to deal with the diversity threatening American culture was to reproduce in the second great wave of immigrants a common American set of values. Southern Europeans of the second wave were viewed as different. Catholic and non-English-speaking, this group prompted the educational leaders to set up night classes in the urban high schools to teach adult immigrants English and citizenship. Each successive cultural group that entered the United States was to be acculturated into this model. No respect or consideration for alternative languages and religious beliefs was manifest.

Cubberley deeply influenced the field of organizational theory and school administration. His many textbooks taught the virtues of managerial control and systemization of all facets of school operations. Under his direction, dissertations on topics as arcane as how to apply floor wax flowed from Stanford's School of Education. Soon the nation was engaging in an orgy of efficiency and organizational effectiveness strategies (Callahan, 1962).

The effect on the school space was to make it a contested ground. Teachers, administrators, and political elites sought to gain control of that school space to advance their own images of schooling. Teachers' unions reacted to the overly managed nature of their work, administrators balked at evaluations of their labor, and politicians and ward heelers sought to use the schools as agencies of graft and corruption. The resulting schools were battlegrounds in which contending interests sought to gain the upper hand.

The Progressive Education Reform

In the latter part of the 19th century, school reforms erupted all over the United States. Through mostly grassroots reforms, schools changed from formal spaces in which silence and obedience were primary and learning secondary to new "progressive schools" where students became the focus once again. "Learn by doing" and "experimental education" were just two of the slogans that identified a shift in philosophy. The school space underwent changes as well. Tables and chairs replaced the student seats screwed to the floor. Projects replaced the rote memorization and copy book exercises. Teachers, appealing to a new progressive approach, emphasized creative work and expression. Professional journals began printing student drawings, and a new emphasis on method was evident everywhere. Diversity was dealt with in two ways during this period.

The melting pot. Israel Zangwill (1914) proposed an alternative to the conformity theory of Mann in the early 20th century. His metaphor was the *melting pot.* Here differing cultural groups were stirred together in a great cauldron of differences from which emerged a new American, different from each particular ethnic group. Sensitivity to cultural heritage and uniqueness was sacrificed for a new cultural homogeneity and social solidarity. A "new American" was prophesied.

Schools came to be administered by school executives dedicated to efficiency and cost effectiveness. Hence questions of ethnicity, gender, race, and religion were sidestepped in the effort to post ledger sheets that balanced. Students exhibiting differences were judged in terms of a new homogenized American. Public relations converted the school into a panacea dedicated to ministering to the diverse populations coming to the American shores while producing a single product—the new American (Callahan, 1962; Perkinson, 1991). However, some groups either refused or failed to melt! What occurred was a relative assimilation of some groups and parts of groups into a type of mainstream American culture, while a reaction relative to nonassimilated groups set in. Urban educational systems began to look very much like contemporary restructured schools. Ethnic communities took over local control of schools through political pressure. In the face of reform, machine politicians resisted professional educators' agendas for strengthening and centralizing administration for the simple reason that they saw the importance of schools as enhancing local social life, rather than raising educational standards or improving the status of educators (Peterson, 1985). Schools functioned as pluralizing agencies that exaggerated difference on the one hand but paid lip service to organizational efficiency and productivity on the other.

During most of the 20th century, people of color, women, and the disabled found the melting pot to be an unworkable metaphor for them in the face of the dominant culture ethos in the United States. Large numbers of people remained invisible and outside the pot.

Cultural pluralism. After World War I, Horace Kallen (1924/1970), a Jewish professor in New York City who had witnessed discrimination firsthand, proposed a new metaphor—*cultural pluralism*. Kallen maintained that each ethnic group must retain its customs and traditions while participating in the society at large. Through the mechanism of *orchestration* these differing elements of culture would be made harmonious.

Fueled by a new liberalism, Kallen (1956) and others attempted to deal with cultural diversity by arguing that schools and school leaders had the responsibility of *cultural mediation*. Schools became a selecting device that extracts from the mix of culture the preferred cultural aspects and passes these on to the children. Beyond this, schools do not just reflect culture; they shape it by choosing certain cultural components for *cultural transmission*.

Much was written of cultural pluralism as a plan. It was tried in the 1930s by the Bureau of Intercultural Education in Washington, DC. Led by Rachael DuBois, the bureau sought to reinforce the identities of certain cultural groups and to counter ethnocentrism and racism in America via publications and education. In practice this progressive effort became entangled in big-city politics. Unable to secure teaching and administrative posts for African Americans in Detroit, the bureau was reduced to a paper-shuffling agency of the government. Diverse groups continued to languish because they did not have strong enough spokespersons or they failed to be identified as part of the public space of schools.

The 1960s

When the Little Rock (Arkansas) schools were desegregated in 1968, Americans suddenly came to realize that difference must be accommodated by the public schools. This event divided the space of the public school into two colors, White and Black. African American children had been invisible until this time. Large numbers of African Americans had migrated to northern cities looking for work after World War II. The public school became a contested ground in which race identified the combatants.

Certainly large numbers of immigrants had been assimilated into the mainstream culture, but here was a population that could not melt because it was visibly different. The notion that issues of race could divide the school now became a reality. It is no surprise that desegregation reached effective levels only when the focus was on elementary and secondary schools. Great in number and in numbers of clients, the public schools drew national attention to lack of integration everywhere.

Ravitch (1983) demonstrated that the means used to achieve racial balance in the public schools was adopted by other groups who were invisible. Disabled youngsters, women, and other groups have used similar methods to achieve balance as well. Courts of law emerged as arenas in which the contestants battling for a share of the public school space could engage in combat. In addition, for the first time, policy makers began drawing on the professional social scientist-researcher as expert witness. Social change was rapid, and even the smallest interest group (e.g., the Amish) could gain national attention through the use of the courts. In the name of equality of opportunity, the social space of the public school took on all the appearances of Flanders Field.

Today

In America today the philosophy of difference asserts that the characteristically different must be accounted for and that schools be arranged to accommodate diverse patrons and their interests. Diverse groups are multiplying as we speak. Postmodern American culture is nothing if it is not a veritable plethora of historical and emerging ethnic, racial, gender, religious, and other interest-driven groups.

However, in the face of diversity in American culture, there are those who preach divisiveness and separateness on the one hand and conformity on the other. In some hands, political correctness descends to a near-ideology of censorship and control of what is said and done relative to The Other. In response to racism, sexism, ageism, sizeism, and so forth, well-meaning intellectuals have created a language of inoffensive terms and anomalous speech that sweeps the problems of interrelationship under the rug, polarizing groups and cutting off communication. At the other extreme, a constellation of "culturecentric" efforts has emerged that attempts to elevate single sets of standards and norms by which all the differing groups are to be measured. E. D. Hirsch's (1987) cultural literacy and William Bennett's (1993) virtues education are examples. On the surface, a narrow band of factual knowledge is equated with American cultural citizenship, although at a deeper level, advocates of such a view root that knowledge in a museum of historical power, privilege, and control.

Both the politically correct and the culturecentric solutions to diversity seek to elevate a pedagogy of uncritical transmission and reproduction of the canon. Together these visions redefine democracy and diversity according to their respective ideologies. The relationship between knowledge and truth is no longer seen as problematic. Instead, cultural institutions are made into an arena of conflict in which adversaries in belief are to be confronted and condemned. Both views stop time and culture to seize on images and metaphors that indemnify their privileged beliefs. Together these solutions to cultural diversity result in a new aristocracy and privilege, new power and authority, new speech and representation— all aimed at marginalizing others and subordinating discourse and practice to ideal categories of acceptability. Any vision of American democracy as a fuller interplay of communicative, intelligent, moral-aesthetic, and communal interests is blurred and distorted from view.

Cultural Diversity as Meaning or Plan?

There are two sides to the complex cultural condition in the United States. The first aspect is that of cultural diversity seen as a set of differences that compose the culture at large. This is cultural diversity as *meaning*. Of course there may be differences in explanation and understanding of cultural differences as they play a part in the larger social life, but these meanings of cultural diversity are increasingly a fact of our existence. Some societies face greater diversity than others (compare the cultures of Japan and Los Angeles). Yet all cultures that are open have some aspects of difference.

Next, cultural diversity exists as a *normative plan*. Cultural diversity may operate as a set of recommendations or an ought—often within schools and in the form of educational curricular programs and teaching strategies of multiculturalism. Too often we confuse the pluralistic condition of culture as a given set of meanings in our lives with the plans and programs for cultural pluralism. One important issue facing American culture illustrates this difference: How are we to accommodate and sustain crucial claims of difference (i.e., cultural diversity as meaning) while recognizing and encouraging emerging culture groups (i.e., cultural pluralism as norm)? Both older and emerging groups seek a place in the culturally diverse society as well as gaining reflections for their own group identity. Implicit in these goals are process values of conformity, difference, reproduction, critique, and so on—all tagged to history, all competing themes of educational structure.

The critical pragmatist rethinks the separation between these two views of culture. The interest moves to (a) reattaching visions of future culture with their respective inquiry structures and frameworks; (b) focusing on the critique of such plans and programs; (c) testing programs of cultural pluralism and their implementation strategies (both potentially and actually); and (d) setting plans against current cultural conditions unhampered by prejudice and discrimination. The key to inscribing a viable cultural diversity for the postmodern future is through the exercise of pragmatic method seen as a set of enabling values of intelligence laid against the backdrop of a set of content values of democratic pluralistic culture—these processes and contents intimately linked in a social way of living.

As we try to come to grips with the disorder in our schools, we need to reflect on historical meanings and plans Americans have embraced to deal with cultural diversity. In this way we may develop a rationale for building a new school order for the next century that is open and free.

Confronting the Chaos of Diversity

Cultural diversity is on the increase. There are more groups and more affiliations than ever before. Religious cults, ethnic and gender collectivities, political and work groups, and so forth have multiplied as American society has lost its central core of beliefs. The modern form this approach has taken is called the theory of *cultural reproduction.* The problem of cultural transmission in the schools is characterized by the concepts of *cultural capital* and *cultural literacy* to chart the processes by which the larger culture was passed on (reproduced) in the schools (Bourdieu & Passeron, 1977). Schools sought to teach the dominant cultural orientation while deemphasizing other, alternative views perceived as "inferior subcultural."

Critics argue that cultural capital was first acquired from the family, but this form of culture might well be suppressed by the school as it sought to transmit the dominant culture. A type of symbolic violence was done as the knowledge and values of the dominant order were set out as both legitimate and necessary for students to acquire. Schools gave the impression that they were neutral regarding the dominant culture while simultaneously enhancing its status. Bourdieu and Passeron (1977) pointed out that it is important to see the role of external interests as they exercise control and direction over the school in the form of the hegemonic curriculum. Differing cultures and subcultures were deemed inferior and were marginalized or rejected in the curriculum and pedagogy.

To view the educational organization as a reproduction device must in every instance express the ideological position embedded in the culture, asserted Bourdieu and Passeron (1977). Following Giroux (1983), Stanley (1992) noted that cultural reproduction casts individual persons as passive recipients of cultural capital. Overly deterministic, the cultural reproduction theory tended to minimize human freedom. Humans are slighted, and self-empowerment is overlooked as an agency for transformation. Reproduction theorists provided little insight into how schools within specific historical contexts accomplished cultural reproduction. Where a contradiction occurred between an individual's cultural *habitus* (internalized needs and competencies of cultural participants) and the institution of the school (*habitat*), changes in that position were deemed a cultural accident and not a result of critical self-reflection. Schools are never just rubber-stamp agencies (hegemonic in nature) satisfying dominant groups: Schooling both conserves and constructs the identity of such groups. Cultural reproductionists overlook the concrete parts of economic domination that produce constraining elements beyond mere symbolic violence. For critical pedagogues such as Henry Giroux (1983), cultural reproduction theory fails to provide for any possibility of resistance to oppressive and disabling facets of the dominant culture (see Stanley, 1992).

Cultural reproduction theory has been countered and improved on by a group of theorists who embrace alternative versions of resistance theory. Apple (1982), Freire (1970a, 1970b, 1970c, 1973, 1985), Freire and Macedo (1987), Giroux (1983, 1985, 1988a, 1988b, 1988c), Shor (1980/1987, 1992), and Willis (1977) have sought to revitalize the examination of education and to promote critical reform in schools (Stanley, 1992).

Resistance theorists such as Henry Giroux and Peter McLaren offer hope for a new border pedagogy that allows educators to refuse to accept older dominant meaning systems (White, Anglo, and male) and the politics of multiculturalism that perpetuates these systems. Instead, the thinkers wish to affirm and legitimate the knowledge-meanings emerging from local communities of differing constellations but at the same time interrogate the interests, ideologies, and practices such knowledge-meanings serve. The ways for so testing local meanings is found in the global world of the economics of power and privilege. Through the vehicle of critical teaching, a "resistance postmodernism" is enacted, liberating repressed individuals and groups. At the heart of this critical pedagogy is a belief in democracy and the allied notion of a public space in which a type of critical citizenship may emerge. Giroux is careful to encourage educators to take up the idea of difference and transform its meaning from cultural essentialism and centrism to new alliance building. By dreaming and imaging together, groups may come to embrace a new solidarity and thus learn to cross borders (McLaren, 1994).

Critical Pragmatism

John Dewey (1916b) spoke of the "hyphenated American," a conception of human life that proposed that it was through interactions with others—joined by ethnic, racial, religious, and other interests—that a person came to be not a single identity but a person having a variety of cultural parts, each drawn from different sources. Moreover, he argued that such a new American was a result of securing and enhancing "interests." Thus it was not so much the extant fact that we were a plural nation but rather that we seized on some meanings for these parts of our distinct cultures to highlight and transmit. Such transmissions were always mediated by present concerns and were partial at best. Schooling ought therefore to provide a rich communal space in which the members emphasize the interests of their respective group. Finally, these interests and consequent affiliations were fluid rather than "in the bone." Dewey saw American society and culture as open and developing, a community of communities in which neither radical pluralism nor cultural centrism could survive in the scheme of things (pp. 183-189).

Thus the critical pragmatic view of diversity accepts the role of culture critic and asks the fundamental question: Why do we think the way we do about schools, and what practical difference do diverse interests make? The school space is contested today but in a different way from the earlier Deweyan world of industrialized capitalistic America. Early modernism and capitalism had served to repress certain groups and interests. Today the demons are different. We must identify the character of contemporary culture in a new struggle to advance freedom over the tyranny of control.

For the critical pragmatist, the role of a quality-sensitive intelligence is paramount in the interrogation of societal conditions. It is premature to specify detailed programs for the resolution of school problems. Critical pragmatists spend more time specifying the procedural norms and operational concepts they consider significant in moving toward solving problems of schools set by diversity.

Critical pragmatists separate themselves from old-style liberals because they favor less the modernist devices of rationality, science, and government to solve problems set by diversity in American society. Early liberals, such as Horace Kallen (1924/1970, 1925), often believed that the political state through its impress on institutions such as the public school could solve the problems of minorities. Schools in the 1920s and 1930s constructed showers, built home economics kitchens, and in other ways sought to teach children and youth principles of good health and social manners. The liberals believed that the schools could solve social problems if given sufficient time and resources. This assumption of human capacity to render discordant into harmonious development is attached to the earliest Western notions of progress.

Politics is operative throughout the social space of schooling. Public and private are not so separate when we view the problems these sectors face. Human associations are wide ranging but share a desire to accomplish their ends. The state has an obligation to aid in the resolution of difficulties throughout the culture. Critical pragmatism is a method more than it is a concrete program of social reform (Anderson, 1990). Relative to school restructuring, pragmatic liberalism does not provide the ideal configuration of diversity for schools but rather the methodological tools for bringing school reconstruction into being.

Critical pragmatism is in sharp disagreement with melting pot, Anglo-Saxon conformity, and other solutions advanced for the paranoia of cultural chaos. It is insufficient to pass on the diversity as it stands because to do so is not to improve on the conditions of those disabled by unequal cultural status. It is likewise unacceptable to simply allow cultural mixing to produce preferred cultural pluralisms for the postmodern future. To do this is to suspend belief in the capacities of human intelligence to improve on the disenfranchised and powerless.

Pragmatism improves on all chaos and conflict theories of culture by focusing more on the harmonies, continuities, and similarities found in cultural group values. Although the other theorists are often trapped by their framework as they seek to locate conflicts within society, critical pragmatists do not favor upsetting established habits and beliefs where these work.

Critiques of Cultural Restructuring

It is possible to find two different types of critique of school restructuring as implementing cultural diversity: (a) internal criticisms and (b) external criticisms. The internal variety of critique is what may loosely be termed in-house evaluations of diversity. The aim is to challenge the operative plan of diversification on the grounds that it fails to adequately fulfill certain core political beliefs. In this version, the political core meanings are not questioned. Disputed is the extent to which the program for diversity fulfills them. One example of this type of criticism is found in Milton Gordon's (1964) *Assimilation in American Life,* in which he criticizes historical plans of cultural pluralism (particularly those of Horace Kallen and Isaac Bergson) for their incompleteness.

A second and perhaps more controversial type of critique is the external appraisal. In this case there is a systematic effort not to retain allegiance to the norms of a particular political philosophy but rather to question the plan for cultural diversity on differing sets of criteria. Robert Paul Wolff in *A Critique of Pure Tolerance* (1969) wrote:

> Pluralism is a theory of the way modern industrial democracies work, with particular applicability to the United States; it is also an ideal mode of the way political society ought to be organized, whether it is or not. As a descriptive theory, pluralism requires empirical verification of the sort which hosts of political scientists have sought to provide in recent

decades. As a normative theory, however, pluralism must be defended by appeal to some principle of virtue or ideal of the good society. (p. 15)

When we examine plans for cultural restructuring, several conditions and features seem evident. First, most normative views of cultural reform favor groups already in existence and are antagonistic toward new groups or associations. It is assumed that hereditary groups are more representative of societal feelings, attitudes, beliefs, and opinions. In concrete practice plans tend to support inequality by ignoring the existence of certain social groups. In effect, plans of diversity may marginalize some members of society (Wolff, 1969).

A second condition of pluralism and diversity is that they often assume government to be an adjudicating agency in regulating competition among groups. However, in practice, government tends to decide among certain recognized power groups while ignoring smaller, less powerful, or less vocal interests. It is further assumed that the individual will be affiliated with one or more groups, accepting the programs and values of these groups. It seems to follow logically that cultural diversity programs entail a high degree of tolerance for diversity, although having little or no tolerance for particular deviant individual persons (Wolff, 1969).

A third condition encountered in plans of cultural diversity is their tendency to discriminate not only against certain social groups and interests but also against certain types of proposals for the solution of social problems. Programs of cultural reform often assume that social problems are problems of one or more groups, not of society at large. Pluralistic lines of thinking tend to overlook the common good of society (Wolff, 1969).

A fourth feature of normative diversity plans is that pluralism both as a program and as a conceptual map functions as a mere extension of older style liberalism. Modern industrial and business groups are substituted for the single individual. These economic groups become the basic unit of societal interaction: "Liberals ground their view of cultural diversity on the assumption society should be composed of groups pursuing their own interests. However, the tendency is to equate 'group' with 'interest' while neglecting the subjective element of interest" (Balbus, 1971, p. 154).

Attached to this difficulty is the fact that it is frequently assumed by diversity advocates that local pluralism is merely a subspecies of federal or national political pluralism. Gitlin (1965) offers an external critique of diversity theory by focusing on this local level. Power is not divided on the local or city level, as traditional pluralist theory seems to assume. Important decisions are often made in private and not in public. In addition, power must be truly shared if liberal democracy is to be operative.

A fifth condition of postmodern society finds important sources of information—information necessary for decision making according to diversity theory—to be unavailable. Persons may be systematically blocked from accessing such information. Governmental secrecy makes an informed decision incomplete. Some decision theorists, such as Herbert Simon (1971), have argued that there is often insufficient time to gather and process such information so that the best course of action may be chosen. Simon maintained that decisions are necessarily "satisficing" in nature. We are never in a position to explore and evaluate all the facts of the case in making up our minds about what we should do.

The sixth condition finds beneath many of the so-called romantic or naturalistic views of cultural diversity a parallel argument or assumption that there must be a loosely coupled central organization. However, in lieu of such a central authority, processes by which conflicts are to be resolved among competing groups are often weak or nonexistent. One of the disadvantages of some plans of cultural diversity is found in the failure to locate or defend appropriate means and agents for resolving intergroup conflict and disagreement.

Last, often programs of cultural diversity do not effectively deal with private action. The distinction between public and private is blurred. Hence it is not clear what a particular group retains by virtue of its character as a group and what individuals retain as part of their private domain.

A New Cultural Democracy

Although culture and cultural diversity are conceptual constructs about societies' and groups' empirical attributes under study, these concepts also see the investigator exercising an active role in bringing about greater understanding. As Smelser (1992) stated: "The process which necessarily occurs in investigating culture should be made explicit in the operation of apprehending it" (p. 23). This is a virtue of pragmatism. Both the inquiry into cultural diversity and the tools allowing the inquiry are open to question.

It is arguable that the degree to which a culture is diverse or unified, chaotic or ordered, is dependent on the framework (theory of culture) used to depict it. The framework is seen as both local and partial in its explanatory value. A cultural description should be assessed primarily on its explanatory adequacy as provocative of concrete experiences and not solely on its logical-structural features (Smelser, 1992). Chapter 1 discussed how important frameworks thinking has been and argued for newer, richer movements that depart from such structured and formal method.

The concepts of culture and cultural diversity may work as heuristic devices functioning as hypotheses for testing against empirical evidence. The concept of cultural diversity ought to be treated not as a global unity but rather as having parts (values, beliefs, ideologies, and preferences). Any researcher's effort to depict culture will yield some measure of incoherence, incompleteness, illogicality, and contradiction. The investigator will encounter individual and social pressures to represent the culture as more coherent or less coherent than it appears. We must be alert to such pressures, and we must see that beyond the issue of the empirical characterization of cultural coherence or incoherence lie nasty matters of social control, social conflict, and social change (Smelser, 1992). The form of culture, then, becomes crucial. Whether it is arranged autocratically or democratically affects diversity.

Contrasting Visions of Democracy

One way to clarify a notion of democracy as being fruitful for dealing with educational reorganization along pluralistic lines is to trace the historical difference between the various liberal philosophies that have dominated social life over time.

Democratic realism. The prevailing notion of *democracy,* which collapsed the descriptive force of the term with the normative or recommendational plan of *democracy,* gained its ascendancy in the 1950s. Political theorists had worked from the 1920s onward to construct an empirical democratic theory. Fearful of the public, realists sought to move decision making out of the hands of the masses and into the hands of specialists. Armed with requisite knowledge and skill, these elites were to be the officeholders of the future. A succession of such elites would govern (Westbrook, 1991).

Participation in public life was not to be direct but rather to be vested in the elites. Although the average person retained some influence over the select few specialists, policy was to be in the hands of experts. Of course elites could manipulate public opinion and retain office, thus negating the power of the public. Democratic realists such as Walter Lippmann were able to show that competition among elites for office would take care of this problem (Westbrook, 1991).

The great fear for the democratic realist was widespread political participation on the part of the public. Stability would be sacrificed when incompetent citizens engaged in political decision making. Interference by citizens was to be discouraged because it would interfere with the friendly competition among elites. In fact, public apathy toward politics was viewed as preferable and as a functional feature of democracy. Even invocations for the public to participate in politics masked the real intent, which was to keep elites behaving properly (Westbrook, 1991).

Democratic realists introduced an ethical shift when they proposed that self-government was not an end in itself but a means toward the end of efficiency in management. The goal was social stability rather than individual growth through participative association, as Dewey argued. As Westbrook (1991) pointed out: "The central political imperative for the realists was to develop a system that was governed effectively and efficiently and retained enough participation to be relatively democratic in a world of more or less authoritarian regimes. For the realists, participatory democracy was not essential to the welfare of the public" (p. 546).

Cultural democracy. In a small volume entitled *What Is Democracy?* written with John Dewey and T. V. Smith, Bode H. Bode (1939) penned an essay called "Ends and Means in Education, or the Conflicts in Our Cultural Heritage." Bode asked what is meant by the term *democracy.* Commonly, the term *democracy* meant to convey a political understanding. Majority rule and the right to vote come to mind when we use the term. Over time, democracy has had other meanings attached to it. The ideas of freedom, equality, and rights have surfaced in the discourse regarding democratic life. Bode argued that such attributions failed to capture what democracy really means. American life in the 20th century was polarized by two forces. On the one side was the pull of the authority of political economy. Pulling on the other side was religious authority. Both these authorities set a barrier to those wishing to invest Americans with the opportunity to enjoy life, liberty, and the pursuit of happiness. As Bode saw it, the conflict was with the absolute nature of these elite authorities.

By the 1930s a new phrase—*cultural democracy*—had been introduced by pragmatists. Bode (1939) wrote:

> If we are to remain a democratic people, we seem to have no choice but to seek maximum development for the individual through the cultivation of a common life and to make the continuous extension of common interests our final test of right and wrong or of what is called progress. (p. 14)

But when Americans sought to act in accordance with this test, they met with the obstacle of traditional theological, political, economic, and ethical absolutes. The central means for overcoming these absolutes and for redefining the standards of democracy to exercise the educational function to reconstruct our way of life lay in critical intelligence.

Bode argued that education must be continuous with the civilization or culture in which it operates. In American civilization, there is a basic conflict between truly democratic norms and the standards of authority. The teacher ought not to decide which of these standards is to win; however, she or he should decide to which to be loyal, for this will form the basis of the entire school program. If one is loyal to democracy, then a reconstruction of society, through the medium of the school, follows. Bode (1937) emphasized, "The primary aim of education is to set intelligence free" (p. xiii). Bode placed special emphasis on the role of reflective thinking in bringing about a settlement of cultural contradictions. Diversity, where it borders on polarization of ideas, is to be fought through the active engagement of intellect with the problems to be solved (Childs, 1956).

Thus, in sharp contrast to the historical elitism of democratic realism, a new postmodern vision of cultural democracy had been launched. Today, political theorists speak of this postliberal and postmodern democracy as participatory democracy (Dryzek, 1990), strong democracy (Barber, 1984), and cultural citizenship (Reyes, 1993). This latter phrase references the right of groups to be different but emphasizes a responsibility to the larger democracy as well. Given this view, differences of race, gender, and so forth are never to be used as the basis for making people unequal or deeming them inferior. Following the cultural citizenship approach to diversity, Reyes has proposed: "We need a new system—a system that calls for a new form of democracy in public schools and in higher education—a democracy which affirms that all people are important and equal and that no culture will be relegated to second class citizenship" (pp. 11-12). This cultural democracy finds students, teachers, administrators, and parents coming together to engage in unfettered dialogue regarding what types of institutions and lives we should aspire to in the future.

Interests and Cultural Diversity

Two types of cultural diversity exist. One version is hierarchical and elitist and may be termed *vertical pluralism*. This type of diversity finds groups isolated from one another, pursuing their own agendas. A second type of pluralism is *horizontal pluralism*. In this mode of cultural patterning, groups have an equal opportunity to formulate and work toward their goals, but competition and critical dialogue (and struggle) between groups may occur.

Calls for ethnic, gender, religious, or any other type of empowerment necessarily link an implicit program of cultural pluralism with social, political, and economic factors. In the face of the search for power in our pluralistic culture, any plan of cultural enhancement must take existing political and economic patterns seriously. We must accept the fact of cultural relativity, although being on guard not to codify this condition. We should seek to move beyond such relativism following reflection. Participants in cultures prize differing components of culture. However, needed is intelligent control of experience so that ways are developed to appraise these prizings. Naive acceptance of cultural interests enslaves us to tradition as an authority, whereas a critical evaluation of interests liberates us. Here we require a theory of reflective practice, or critical pragmatism, aimed at the scrutiny of cultural meanings to test them against experience. Relativity must not be elevated into an ideology of close-minded acceptance of traditional values (romanticism). Ways must be found to communicate across differences. Intercultural conflict is a significant barrier to understanding. In the present instance, we need an open, communicated expression of values to create shared and common concerns for harmoniously accomplishing interest-driven goals.

In principle, a diversity of cultural meanings need not deny the shared acceptance of process values. It is not incompatible in practice to have a cultural pluralism and an integration of method. But even before such a compatible confluence of value-meanings emerges, we must admit that the capacity of pluralisms is comparable in nature. Promoting transcultural values of a process type to include comparing does not lead to the breakdown of subgroup identity. In the long run, we move beyond cultural relativity (with its varied richness) and promote cooperative, transcultural efforts for sociopolitical continuity and development as well. Each minority interest may come to see its own uniqueness and worth realized through interactions and transactions with other groups. Here the mechanism of communication provides the avenue through which differing ethnic and other interest groups may share in mutual understanding.

A wide variety of meanings may be considered as preparatory to the discussion of cultural democracy and the schools. These cultural meanings are narrative, icons, ritual, and ethos. Viewed from an anthropological perspective, such cultural creations as myths, paintings, plays, and moral-ethical character traits form a type of glue that confers identity to groups and continuity and comparability to the culture at large. School leadership has opportunities to incorporate myths and folktales into the day-to-day operations of the school. Unfortunately, the public character of education in the United States has led to a nonsectarian Protestant belief system that is resistant to cultural contents of rival groups. There is a need to introduce cultural folkways into the schools and to teach students about them.

In sum, cultural democracy has attached to it process ideas and cultural meanings that together make it a desired way of designed living. Although in the past actual democracy was defined by one person-one vote, trial by jury, and representative government, in the postmodern world these virtues somehow miss the real meaning of democracy. We must have a more fundamental set of commitments. Next is a closer look at these democratic values.

Process Values

The key values of our notion of cultural democracy for the schools are located in the virtues of the critical pragmatic process. I have identified these as the following: communication, aesthetic-intelligence, and community.

Communication. Communication forms one of the criterial methods of this new democracy. Dialogue and conversation are pledged to the value of continuous discussion and debate, not only regarding the ends but also regarding the means of reaching goals. Openness is related to the discourse value. As a process value, discursiveness is taken to be intimately connected to practice (discourse-practice) rather than being antecedent to practice. In the new leadership, it is argued that dialogue is a learned process and must be carried into professional work. Ira Shor (1992) in *Empowering Education: Critical Teaching for Social Change* pointed out that needed in empowerment is a "third idiom," a dialogue of teaching and learning that simultaneously is concrete and conceptual, academic as well as conversational, yet critical and accessible (pp. 254-255). I add that this third idiom is necessarily an ethnohumanistic dialogic that embraces everyday life in democratic context as a form of art that emancipates, enriches, and enlarges our experience. The effort is one of seeing diverse interests and desires of persons and groups as mutually reinforcing and important; it also seeks to provide a critical design for their emergence and sustenance.

Aesthetic-intelligence. This complex identifies a most inclusive process value of democracy. Critical pragmatism as a method of intelligence driven by a concept of artful practice has historical roots in the ideas of John Dewey, John L. Childs, Kenneth Benne, and R. Bruce Raup. Key ingredients of this method are (a) the emancipation of critical human inquiry and the embrace of experimentalism; (b) edification (through artistic perception in the present instance); (c) emphasis placed on ends-in-view, fruits, and results; (d) the denial of metanarratives and absolutes; and (e) a rejection of all dualisms (Maxcy, 1991).

The new school democracy must release us from the historical desire to base executive administration in some set of absolute ideals or metanarratives. This desire hampered and stilted growth. School leaders must be alert to the idealists' efforts to introduce paralyzing structures that fail to guide living designs but serve as marginalizing ends in themselves. A nonfoundational view assumes there are no once-and-for-all ideals by which competing interests are to be judged. Each conflict is to be resolved through the best pragmatic means available while working toward the ideal of freedom.

Community. Community is another vital component of the new muscular democracy. Unity, solidarity, and cohesiveness are three allied values that serve critical administrative practice. Following Rorty (1989), it is proposed that one of the key values of any group is communal cohesiveness. In stark contrast to the chaos of schools in some inner-city settings, leaders must see ways to critically appraise the divisive and discordant with an eye to growth of conjoint and cooperative living.

A new search for a communal space called *school* is under way. Schools are microcommunities and as such they require nurture. The leadership must listen to followers, pay attention to service, and provide a "soft touch" in dealing with unformed learners. Community and collective practice is superior to individual ego gratification.

I argue here for the rethinking of democracy so that it provides a open channel to emancipatory educational leadership. This pattern of cultural democracy is social and political, but beyond this it is a way of orchestrated ethical living that is dedicated to human freedom, critical inquiry, and the testing of ideas against the fabric of experience.

Cultural Meanings

Cultural meanings are the multiple and shared ways of living and working, the artifacts of such experiences, and the reflections on such experiences. Where we deal with culture, it is possible to locate these within the broad categories of narratives, icons, rituals, and ethos (Firestone & Wilson, 1985).

Narratives

Stories of all types are important to cultures. One type of story is the myth. Myth may be interpreted in a number of ways. It is vital to see myth not as irrational belief but as a device that sustains a culture group. Instructional leaders, in culturally diverse settings, must be shown the many ways in which myth may be incorporated into curriculum and teaching. Here the school librarian, language arts teacher, and resource person may be of great value. The role of the core of the university preparation program in this regard is not only to teach educator-leaders the narratives of their resident culture but also to teach what narratives are and how they function to integrate a culture and move people to actions.

The different narratives that emerge in ethnic, racial, and other group histories are resources for group identity. These expressions serve leadership as a means of communicating across cultures the variety within the similar. It should also be evident that new schools will develop their own myths and folkloristic wisdom. Myth making is a creative act and must be recognized as important in the identification of self and community. All too often cultural anthropologists and philosophers have neglected the *myth-building* side of cultural membership for the sake of *myth finding*. However, the Nazi

Aryan superiority myth proved to be just such a myth construction that had worldwide consequences for the future of peace. Building new myths that are at once humanistic and culturally enhancing is the trick for school leadership in fragile communities.

Icons

The cultural creative impulse produces artifacts. Many of these artifacts are pictures. One cannot travel in a large city without being struck by the graffiti painted on expressways, subways, and trains. The surfaces of so much of our public space are decorated by spray can and brush.

Rather than seeing these symbols as evidence of deviance in our youth, it is better to realize the impulses driving such expressions. All cultures have manifested icons of one sort or another. These symbols of culture tend to rally support for ideas or express repressed interests. Schools that marshal the artistic impulse and channel it into culturally important media are contributing to both the sustenance of culture and the development of immature creative abilities.

Bernal and Knight (1993) have studied ethnic identity and the roles of social scientists in government as they create and sustain multicultural policies, with resultant ethnic group responses to such philosophies and governing rules. Pride in origins may be instilled but against a current of managed efficiency and artificial harmony. Church-state separation was never meant to cleave cultures into diverse parts. Religious beliefs and rituals infuse public art. It is vital to surface these non-co-opting cultural icons and to draw on them to link the students, teachers, and parents in an aesthetic and moral school community.

Rituals

Ritual is everywhere in every culture. Here again the educator-leader is in a prime position to introduce rituals drawn from sub-culture groups. School plays and choral and band recitals provide opportunities to draw on traditional drama, music, and dance. Peter

McLaren (1993) has written persuasively regarding the use of rituals to critically confront dominance of one culture over another. Culturally integrating values may be taught and reinforced via these means. Imber-Black and Roberts (1992) illustrated how we may tap the power of ritual to express values, heal old wounds, and deepen human relationships. Daily rituals of greeting, parting, and mealtime activities offer opportunities to develop cultural awareness and uniqueness. Celebration rituals (birthday, anniversary, etc.) may be seized on to enhance multicultural meanings.

As Dewey argued, it is vital to retain cultural meanings as well as promote cross-cultural process values. Variations such as dress and lifestyle are not held to be incompatible with the democratic process values. It is important that new patterns of cultural richness and diversity are to be based on freer association formed out of human interest and shared concern. Envisioned through cultural democracy is an open society of freely formed and forming interest groups.

Ethos

The concept of ethos also allows us to decipher pluralistic cultures. For if critical pragmatism is pledged to the conscious and critical reconstruction of democratic culture, then there is a tandem need for cultural moral-ethical character—a type of moral artistry. It is not enough to think of the aesthetically proper design for cultural participation; one also needs to test this out in practical choices. These choices rest on the value of freedom over that of control.

Leadership that possesses moral character is the type of moral-ethical rectitude that requires administrators, managers, and coordinators to "stay the course," or "stay with the ship." Character is a matter of values achieved through nurturing, development, and tested experience. Cultural identity carries with it this potential for character growth. Programs in educational leadership must be alert to the need for building a moral-ethical atmosphere in the school, a space in which these elements of character are developed in children and youth through interesting curricula and teaching methods.

Cultural Interests in Democracy

The philosophic grounds for understanding culture as we find it and for more adequately devising plans of cultural diversity for the postmodern future are vital to success in reordering America's schools. Following is a look at one subcultural group, Hispanic Americans, to detail the bearings that critical pragmatism and cultural democracy may have on it.

Preparing Hispanic American Leaders for the New Democratic School

In all complex cultures, the density of changes increases markedly as the cultures encounter one another. The present culture clusters of Hispanic Americans in the United States are at the threshold of greater complexity. The present moment offers a relatively simpler setting than will afford itself years or decades hence. Planning for a critical cultural democracy is therefore essential if results are to be forthcoming. There are a number of strategic moves that may be made. The most logical is focused on leadership preparation in universities.

Universities have lagged behind efforts to prepare minorities for leadership roles in American institutions. Although academic scholars have done much to dispel the myths attached to race, ethnicity, and gender, they have held to historically undemocratic, anachronistic, rigid, and dysfunctional practices in their treatment of minorities (Trueba, 1993). Required is a concerted effort to build programs that place leaders in multicultural school settings with the problem-solving skills and sensitivities needed to improve the condition of the minority culture and enhance its contributions to society at large.

Sleeter and Grant (1985) located at least five approaches to multicultural education: (a) teaching the culturally different; (b) using human relations and assimilationist methods; (c) single-group studies to promote cultural pluralism by raising consciousness; (d) teaching multiculturalism within the regular curriculum to reflect diversity; and (e) promoting multiculturalism as well as social reconstructionism to encourage students to challenge inequality and promote cultural diversity. Educational leadership programs, following multiculturalism curriculum projects, have neglected the last approach. Leadership preparation must be underwritten by a multicultural understanding that is knowledgeable of culturally plural American society as well as skilled in critically pragmatic cultural reconstruction.

Building Cultural Democracy

Educational leadership preparation programs vary, but a number have infused critique with sensitivity-raising to cultural diversity. Several years ago, the University of Kentucky embarked on a challenging new doctoral program in educational leadership specifically sensitive to the multiple metanarratives underwriting school administration today. Doctoral students are provided theoretical positions and are allowed to judge for themselves which are most fruitful. African American culture courses and theory courses go hand in hand to introduce a new leadership model into Kentucky schools. Miami University of Ohio has constructed a leadership program that rests heavily on critical pedagogy and leadership aimed at marginalized groups. Candidates are placed in schools and return to the university for foundational courses addressing matters of ethics, equity, and difference. Louisiana State University in Baton Rouge has launched a new doctoral program for leaders in higher education that emphasizes counseling skills. The assumption is that college and university administrators require personnel communications preparation above all. The University of Texas at San Antonio school leadership doctoral program seeks to prepare Hispanic American leaders for schools in south Texas.

No matter which program one considers, it typically reflects the preparations, research specialties, and expertise of the faculty, the perceived skill levels and needs of the population to be served, time and structural considerations, professional accrediting agency guidelines, and the sociopolitical constraints of the university and the larger community. Emerging from these considerations, the new educational leadership programs typically draw on three types of knowledge for the future—knowledge of liberal arts and sciences, knowledge of the social sciences, and knowledge of education.

Special attention must be paid to how people learn (educational psychology, special education), how people relate (counseling), and how people make sense of their situation and improve on it (foundations). Democratic leadership rests on a strong understanding of the ways in which we come to know. The new leadership is highly transactional; thus knowing how to dialogue and communicate are vital. Restructured schools reflect on the types of preparation administrators receive in university programs so that theoretical-philosophical meanings are allowed to emerge in school leadership decision making.

It is important to distinguish (as most academic programs do not) educational leadership from educational administration and educational management. Leadership is the transactional discourse-practice involving moral artistry that develops alternative designs of the good school. Lodged in collectivities and moved by communication and collegiality, persons as they engage in leading find they are servants rather than bureaucrats, teachers rather than generals. Leadership always has connected with it educational vision, but such vision is grounded in real-world designs growing from the life of the community and relating back to such community (Maxcy, 1991).

Cultural chaos-order is a natural condition and calls for a philosophy of leadership appropriate for leading institutions in such a complex culture. The school leaders may be instructed in the means by which the school becomes an advocate for the Hispanic American culture. Reaching out through partnerships with the larger community is necessary. The leaders must be school ambassadors, but beyond this they offer the larger community a vision of what pluralism may provide in the way of rich diversity. Placing Hispanic American students in the world of making and using is one possible outcome. Such partnerships are not intuitively arrived at. University programs for educators must be alert to pedagogical means for their realization.

The goal of school leadership preparation in a cultural democracy should be a critical design-practice that avoids the historical penchant to control teachers, children, and school life in general and that enhances freedom of thought and performance. Through the interrogation of cultural meanings, the leaders seek to expand the horizon of understanding via a continuous conversation. A critical pragmatism provides exposure to Hispanic American culture and offers the raw data of tradition and experience as anticipatory of cultural praxis of two sorts: (a) cultural action in the form of conscious reconstruction of meanings and (b) cultural action as transaction and reconstruction. In the latter phase of cultural democratic action, the goal is one of understanding conditions and remaking them through positive contributions to the Hispanic students and society at large.

Hispanic American Cultural Meanings

Narratives: Myths and tales. Oscar Hijuelos's Pulitzer prize-winning novel *The Mambo Kings Play Songs of Love* (1989) and the writings of Sandra Cisneros and Julia Alvarez have opened the world of American art and writing to Latinos. Textbook companies have recently begun to include Latino writers. This trend will improve over time. Required is a redirection of attention to the rich art and literature of Hispanics. The importance of providing artistic resources is twofold: First, these stories may help children and parents identify with their own upbringing. A consciousness emerges. Second, these stories aid Hispanic Americans in traversing their own bicultural terrain. A method of action grows out of this cultural literacy. In the struggle to maintain one's own identity in a pluralistic culture, art and literature are vital. Beyond this, such artists and writers provide a means by which the culture and cultural literacy may grow into new forms. The next generation of Hispanic Americans is shaped by the narratives of yesterday and today.

Icons. One source of designs and texts on which to build a critical democratic practice is the new wave of Hispanic American art. This pictorial heritage will enrich the capacities for understanding and the prospects of community-society contributions of Hispanic Americans.

Viewed from a teaching perspective, Hispanic American visual and literary artistry provides depictions of ethnocultural contributions and membership, as well as yielding evidence for problem posing and dialogue. Folk art provides a rich resource for teaching children and parents the importance of daily activities in realizing cultural dreams. Touring art displays may be brought into the school. Art work reproductions can be checked out of the school library. Teachers must be encouraged to use cultural art forms to lift the spirits of Hispanic Americans and reinvigorate community.

School leadership as an art form offers one of the best means for achieving the possibilities of the new age. This move is in contradistinction to visions of other theorists (e.g., Hodgkinson, 1991; Sergiovanni, 1992) who see leadership solely in morality. Doubtless leading involves morals, but theories of moral leadership tend to be reactionary and hobbling. The tendency is to use morals and moralisms to justify administrator behavior after the fact. On the other hand, art has the potential to release vision and allow for freedom to engage in playfulness. Difficulties attached to conceptualizing vision as arising in the administrators' mind result in the major obstacle to be getting followers to accept their vision. Vision as art involves composing and designing as well as decomposing and redesigning. The difference between an executive visionary and an artist is the fundamental source and rational justification of the vision. Both the Machiavellian autocrat and the cultural democratic leader may have visions, but the latter see these as aesthetic constructs and not as intuitive insights into absolute ideals and plans. Artistic visions are tentative and plastic constructions, plural and partial. Machiavellian visions are fully formed personal, intuitively derived plans and programs. The artist composes the vision and communicates it through malleable media on three-dimensional canvases; the autocrat dictates and unfolds fully formed, linear, noncontestable, and engineered blueprints.

Rituals. Viewed from an ethnological standpoint, power and empowerment are characteristics of transactions among cultural participants. Rites and rituals play out conferral dramas of power and empowerment to sanction rule and law. Courtroom judge and attorney, minister and priest, teacher and principal—each engages in culturally sanctioning actions that confer power and empower. These behaviors must be seen in their ceremonial face. (Awarding diplomas at graduation ceremonies, for example, is a sanctioning activity that empowers the learner to practice his or her skills or trade.) It is vital for those engaged in the preparation of school leaders to see the role of awards, certificates, honors, and other badges of arrival and to see the ceremonial nature of such entitlements of power. Terminological, linguistic specifications (master teacher, lead teacher, etc.) are more manifestations of the cultural import of empowerment as a ceremonial device to authenticate professional praxis. We must be alert to these devices, and their influences on school leaders, and the authenticity they lend to the conduct of Hispanic American education.

Ethos. The Hispanic American school must be prepared to aid the larger community in coming to know its ethos. The school leadership is in a unique position as an ambassador of the school to connect the school to the community. The university must prepare leaders for this new type of leadership. Critical cultural democracy leadership revolves around the constructive and integrative use of stories, art, and ritual performance. Leading the community of the Hispanic American school toward a reconstruction of experience in order to enrich the personal lives of participants while simultaneously improving society at large is the ethical ideal of a truly cultural democracy.

Conclusions

A new vision of democracy as a personal and social way of living—a cultural democracy—has been set out for consideration in the preceding pages. This vision is invigorated by the value of diverse communicated interests, the creation of social spaces (schools), the employment of artistic-intelligent design, and the need for a communal impulse of solidarity and cohesiveness. But most significant, our new school space is fueled by a belief in the virtue of freedom over that of control. Cultural democracy ought to replace structured and manipulated old-style liberal, democratic realist organization. We should be able to aid Hispanic Americans and other minorities in gaining control and direction over their identities, unleashing new self-understanding, and propelling vital contributions to community and nation by (a) taking seriously ethnic, racial, and other interests in our society; (b) developing a university program for the preparation of school leaders that builds on knowledge and sensitivity to diversity as well as critical pragmatic approaches; and (c) reenforcing such content and process norms through educational leadership.

In the foregoing it can be seen that the meanings of cultural diversity in the United States are insufficient warrant for any particular plan for school restructuring. The differences attached to pluralisms as facts of culture and to plans or programs of cultural pluralism have been sharply drawn. Required is a new set of metaphors for redressing the diverse grievances while capitalizing on the inherent strengths and uniquenesses in diversity. This chapter has spoken of a critically pragmatic philosophy of social and cultural life that provides norms and instruments for the reconstruction of educational space. This pragmatic approach has been distinguished from other versions of liberalism. It has two types of values attached to it: The first is a set of assumptions regarding the way societal and cultural life is configured; the second is a way of dealing with the problems a pluralistic socioculture sets for us.

Contemporary discussions of school restructuring lack an aesthetic-moral concern, a responsibility-driven interest that would allow groups to prosper in more artfully conceived social spaces. Were such a conception of critically pragmatic postliberalism given free rein in the contemporary arena of school reconstruction, a greater degree of democracy would necessarily invade processes through which plans and proposals for educational rebuilding would emerge. The central problem in school restructure is not an absence of perceived solutions but a lack of commitment to schools as social spaces in which people may engage in artful practices that are at once free and diverse. We must replace the mentality of control with that of a freeing of a social way of living that enhances the capacity to learn to live artful lives.

6

Moral Artistry
in the New School

It is devastating news! School restructuring is not working. Yet another reform has failed to fulfill expectations for a dramatic recovery of American schools. There is little wonder in it, however. The school restructuring effort, like its predecessor reforms, has become ensnared in the metaphysics of structuralist and modernist language and practice. Now is the time for us to employ *moral artistry* (Fesmire, 1994).

Assessments of school restructuring almost invariably highlight the failure of school change when measured against traditional rational and technical norms. The irony may be that school restructuring is succeeding, only against quite different measures. The psyche of Americans today is divided in two. The mind is said to be dominated by one or the other of two brain hemispheres. On the one side is the logical and linear thinking that yields science and mathematics; on the other side is the artistic, offering beautiful paintings and sculptures (Shlain, 1991). For too long we have allowed the legacy of scientific reason to determine our understanding of schools, while leaving silent and unseen the dramatic renditions of educational space that art could provide.

Given the shift toward a postmodern culture, mechanical and artificial yardsticks fail to capture the qualitative changes going on in schools and culture today. Beyond this, it seems evident that a gradual shift from modes of thinking to artistic vision is revealing these qualities and seeking to expose them to the light. Of course, whether educational researchers and reformers see these is crucial. If the present guardians of organizational culture refuse to admit the emergence of a postmodern, poststructural American culture, we may find ourselves in either a full-scale educational revolution or a total collapse of public education as we have known it.

Hence the remarks to follow are crucial for school leadership—students, teachers, parents, and administrators. A new vision is required that will make sense of the diversity versus singularity, frames versus processes of inquiry, chaos versus order, authoritarian versus democratic, and culturally diverse versus culturally solidified school order. Critical pragmatism provides this perspective as it at once critiques the established modes of thinking and the problems of schooling and evaluates ends and means as products of methodologies driven by concerns for communication, intelligence-design, and community. In earlier chapters I have spoken only tangentially of the role of aesthetics in all of this. It is time to explore more in depth this unseen ingredient in school reform.

With a new look at our schools as spaces intersected by competing planes of value-meanings, we must learn to design this space so that it is free, open, and democratic. In so doing, we must become moral artists of sorts, who through our most creative and intelligent deliberation and practical judgment recover the moral ideal of democracy. Much of what is good in schools is overlooked, and much that is wrong is revealed by present frameworks and inquiry methods. Our creative possibilities have been missed by linguistic descriptions of education as engineered and bureaucratically operated businesslike enterprises. Even when we seek to consider the value dimensions of education, we lapse into the language of engineering and technology. We have, as a nation of educators, slipped from our moral principles, forgotten our language of beauty and goodness—yet we cannot understand why our schools fail us.

It is thus no surprise that we are unsuccessful in our effort to restructure schools. Businesses have been restructuring their innards, reengineering their markets, and so have schools—but schools are not businesses: They have different moral ideals, different moral-aesthetic qualities, and different goals. Only by refocusing our artistic eye on the moral landscape of schools will we be able to design more adequately.

We are accustomed to think and talk of organizational effectiveness, organizational behavior, and organizational rules, roles, and relationships. We rarely characterize schools in aesthetic terms. Human feelings and aesthetic vision seem to be on hold. Throughout this book I stress the need for a different approach to school reform in this country. The assumed structures and frameworks to view these are part of the problem. A geometric mentality defines schools as boxes filled with 25 to 35 students, each with a teacher attached. My recommendation is to do away with frameworks thinking and get into the schools as living worlds. I have demonstrated that gross assumptions about the nature of schools and their organization—that they are in chaos—misrepresent the conditions there. Required is a new form of community that reinvents democracy. We need an open philosophy, one that we have never fully embraced in all the history of education in this country. We must see that plans for culturally dividing our nation through schooling in multiculturalism are more often than not imprecise and incomplete—if not totally wrongheaded.

Is it not time to talk about the qualitative aspect of schools as social arrangements? Can we find a way of specifying a more adequate means of school reform? Are we not tired of hearing that schools must redirect their goals in response to schools having become ineffective, impersonal organizations? A new, aesthetic-moral-ethical school is needed. Unfortunately, school reforms continue to focus on problems of governance and organizational structure. How shall we reform education in more aesthetic ways?

The search for an artistic basis on which to reconstruct our schools must be reflected in efforts to develop a critically pragmatic study of chaos and aesthetic-moral-ethical meanings in school culture. This chapter seeks to detail the ways in which we may come to talk and act relative to value beliefs-practices as educators, parents, and students. As part of this concern, the discussion raises the question: How may we come to *see* schools as spaces to be invested with beauty and goodness? How can we "unframe" (rather than "reframe") educational communities and leadership? The answers to these questions must derive from new inquiries, for there is strong modernist and structuralist resistance to educational change. If we but work at it pragmatically, both theoretically and practically, we may better understand moral artistry as it plays on the texture of school life.

Experience

Earlier in this text, the importance of experience in education was noted. A pragmatist begins with a commonsense world. Perceptual qualities are not subjective data used to quantify things, but rather they are immediately experienced qualities of things. Some philosophers talk of this common-sense world as made up of "sense data." This is to assume experience waits for human interactivity. This was not the case for John Dewey (1926/1958), who expressly stated that inquiry is the interaction between an organism (human or other) and the environment. At this primary level, natural occurrences involving humans and the environment occur. These experiencings are not "known," but rather "had." What transforms an experience into a knowing experience is the necessity of a problem and the role of logical thinking (intelligence) in resolving that problem. For Dewey things are had and used before they acquire meaning.

How does an educational experience differ from other sorts of experiences? What are teachers trying to accomplish when they educate? Is there an inclusive educational moment bracketed out from other periods in our lives? What types of experiences ought to provide the means for satisfying our objectives and goals of schooling? How may the school administrator use school theory to maximize the educative experiences of the school? These and other questions focus on the essential unit of education—the educative experience—and matters of direction and fruitfulness.

Experience for John Dewey (1926/1958) was the result of an interaction between objective conditions and organic energies. The educative experience, as a special type of experience, involved the use of experimentation to bring about a resolution of a problem. Dewey's famous problem-solving paradigm for the schools resulted from this insight. The teacher was to be a guide in helping students work through a problem to its solution. In the process of problem solving, students gained skill at instrumentalist thinking. Dewey saw intelligence being applied to an experience to refine and direct it toward a good end. The product of such a process of intelligence is meaning.

From a philosophic standpoint, the experience was the elemental unit. Experiences were had in very fundamental ways. Each person interacts with the world at this elemental experience level. Moreover, each and every experience begins with a resident qualitative aspect. Although an experience may profit from the addition of intelligence and yield knowledge, that experience begins with quality as an earmark. Influenced by Charles Sanders Peirce's (1934/1963a) notion of quality as firstness, Dewey (1934) adopted the notion that value resides in every experience but must be translated through intelligence via appraisal and evaluation. The primary tendency as human creatures is to like, value, and in other ways warmly attend to some things and events rather than others. The reason for this primal reaction is that quality forms an essential ingredient within such experiences.

There are two broad categories of experience, Dewey (1934) argued: Ordinary experience, which is chaotic, unconsummated, and unfulfilling, and *an* experience, which is consummatory and aesthetic. Most experiences, unfortunately, are simply dead ends. There is no significant continuity of one aspect of the experience to the next, and the experience leads nowhere. But *an* experience has a freely flowing motion without sacrifice of any of its parts or their individual identities. The whole experience thus comes to have a unity, an internal integration that overarches the experience. *An* experience is a consummation and has an aesthetic dimension.

By so defining *an* experience as aesthetic, Dewey (1934) leads us to conclude that art is pervasive in all of human life. What makes an experience aesthetic is the interest and purpose that prompts and monitors it through time. An aesthetic experience is one that has the aim of producing or appreciating aesthetic quality. This aesthetic quality in a consummatory experience is a by-product, but in an aesthetic experience itself, this quality is in the forefront. In this way the work of art (painting, sculpture, etc.) is filled with quality of an aesthetic sort.

In *Experience and Nature* John Dewey (1926/1958) called for a philosophy of empirical naturalism. He wished to emphasize the importance of paying attention to the connection between experience and nature. He found that too often traditional philosophies, "in casting aspersions on the events and objects of experience, . . . deny the power of common life to develop its own regulative methods and to furnish from within itself adequate goals, ideals and criteria. Thus in effect they claim a private access to truth" (p. 38).

Dewey (1926/1958) maintained that experiences in the world of empirical matters are uncertain, unpredictable, uncontrollable, and hazardous. We have fear because the world is perilous and precarious. On the other hand, there are regularities and continuities in nature. The change of the seasons, the tides, and other events lend a predictability and flow to life that suggests order, not chaos. The fallacy of philosophy has been to elevate either the regular and recurring or the transient and chaotic. Aristotle, for example, became stuck on the fixed or eternal. The new science of chaos has sought to impute order beneath the chaos—both views seem excessive.

Value Approaches to Organizational Life

Most of the research and writing about schools stresses their organizational features and fails to take moral, ethical, religious, and aesthetic values seriously, or seeks to reduce them to mere matters of fact. Recently, however, experts in school organization theory have come to speak of schools as possessing cultures and climates (Hoy & Miskel, 1991). This admission has opened the school up to new possibilities for research. The older structuralist and popular way of dealing with organizational life has been to reduce it to a set of variables and then, using quantitative measures, determine the relative impacts of these on one another. Value-driven inquiry, often termed qualitative or naturalistic research, seeks to characterize the virtuous school, the moral school, and the aesthetic school.

Instrumental and Intrinsic Value

Philosophers historically divided values into instrumental values and intrinsic values. This dichotomy has been set out in advance and hence misconstrued to confer on values a locus and power that is not borne out in experience. An educational aim, it is argued, is an instrumental value because it is seen as a means to an end. For example, we may say that learning civics is an instrumental value to the intrinsic end of being a good citizen. Citizenship here is a value in itself and does not lead to anything else.

The difficulty with this type of thinking is evident on inspection, for it is possible to argue that any particular value is both an instrumental and intrinsic value. We could make a case for good citizenship being instrumental to leading a good life, for example. The instrumental versus intrinsic distinction is largely context driven. We tend to value some ideas as instrumental in one context and as intrinsic in other situations. This division introduces a pragmatic dimension to our talk of values and aims. Thus we are encouraged to speak of instrumental values and aims and to look at their fruitfulness in future experience. General aims for the school become excuses for certain methods over others. Teachers ought to be concerned with the more focused aims instead.

Value helps us lend meaning to our experiences. Moral, ethical, aesthetic and other types of values will transfer meaning to unformed and elliptical experience.

Over time three orientations have dominated thinking regarding morals and ethics in culture: First, it was taken to be the task of normative language to form itself around principles or rules as a guide to value practice. This deontological view was caught up in Kantianism, various social contract theories, and utilitarianism, for example. The fundamental assumption was that matters of value could be decided based on intersubjectively agreed-on principles. Being moral and ethical was abiding by rules.

The second historical orientation took a different slant. Theorists in this school of thought proposed that normatives were not so much a matter of following rules as a matter of possessing good character. In this mode of thinking, an ethics of virtue was proposed, and teachers in the schools were given the role and responsibility of building such character. This second orientation has died off and reemerged over the decades.

The third orientation toward moral-ethical value matters has its roots in desire theory. This tradition, currently exemplified by the works of Noddings (1984), Gilligan (1982), and others, focuses on caring but is actually tied to certain Western and non-Western theories of morals and ethics.

Unfortunately, school restructuring proposals continue to focus on the logic of governance rather than organizational form. The organization seems resistant to talk of moral agents or ethical leaders redirecting education. Let us look at four proposals for value-based schools.

The Virtuous School

Of recent note is the growing perception that ineffective school organizations are suffering from an absence of morality and ethical standards. Educational theorists Sergiovanni (1992) and Hodgkinson (1991) maintained that if we are to get to the heart and soul of school improvement, we shall require moral leadership. Sergiovanni argued that effective schools "have virtuous qualities that account for a large measure of their success" (p. 99). He identified the "virtuous school" as having a "covenant community" that bonds people in a moral relationship to a common cause or purpose (pp. 108-109). The school covenant of shared values makes for a moral community, with a collective mindscape or world view made up of two types of qualities: basic and temporal. The basic qualities of the covenant are the cherished beliefs regarding the nature and structure of the universe, one's place in it, the nature and purposes of human existence, conceptions of knowledge and the human capacities to acquire it, the nature of human nature (free will, goodness, selflessness, and compassion), the best ways to structure human relationships, and definitions of morality. The temporal qualities of the covenant are such matters as how the school works; the nature of human motivation, power, and authority; how decisions are made; assumptions about how students learn, grow, and develop; and the nature of the schooling process. Sergiovanni punctuated his argument with the claim that schools without covenants, or schools made in the image of organizations, rather than communities, still follow some moral code but that this connection is ill-defined.

On the political New Right, Alasdair MacIntyre (1981), Chester Finn (1991), and, more recently, moral fundamentalist William J. Bennett (1993) have come to speak of the necessity of recovering, teaching, and investing our institutions with our lost moral virtues. The argument to reinfuse old-time moral virtue into the school finds that classical philosophy (MacIntyre, 1981) or 19th-century American McGuffey Reader-like ideals (Bennett, 1993) appeal to the traditionalist and members of the Far Right. Many Americans welcome the idea of recovering lost moral virtues and investing our institutions with them. However, beneath the rhetoric of this moral recovery can be found a devastating criticism of democracy and public schooling. These New Right critics seek to restore moral authority and rigid discipline—all at the expense of cultural diversity, social justice, and democracy. In the final analysis, the virtuous school is really the old-time, little red schoolhouse of our colonial past, and the philosophy is one of Puritanism.

The Caring School

One answer to the question of moral-ethical vacuousness is found in the call for more caring by everyone involved with teaching and learning in schools (Beck, 1994; Noddings, 1984; Sergiovanni, 1992). We are told that what we seriously lack in schools, educational administration, and the preparation programs for principals in particular is an ethic of care (Beck, 1994). This caring forms a piece of the effort to reform organizational life in the schools. The task is not a small one. Among those who embrace caring as a component of school leadership, differing viewpoints regarding the existence, efficacy, and point of caring in schooling are emerging. Scholars have made an articulate and compelling argument for locating and adopting an ethic of care in the contemporary chaos that engulfs American schools.

In educational reforms—whether to improve student performance, solve social problems, or create new modes of school governance—caring is often seen at the center of effort (Beck, 1992). Caring seems to lend itself to the interdependent relationships found in institutions such as schools. Caring flourishes in communal environments. Caring is multidimensional because it has a goal, intentionality, and action dimensions. Caring has a role where administrators face anarchy in schools (Beck, 1992, 1994).

The economic notion that schools are driven by market forces is different from the ideal of schools in which students, teachers, and administrators are treated caringly as persons. Furthermore, where schools and administration must deal with social problems, the effort has historically been focused on balancing quality and equality, while trying to develop virtues. Beck (1992) proposed that instead of straddling the fence on this dichotomy, educators should engage in a commitment to the needs of students and not seek to address large-scale social problems that are beyond the schools' capacity to resolve.

Administrative structures are seen as essentially bureaucratic; efforts to interact are manipulative and authoritarian. By relocating care in the center of such structures, we find a positive attribution to people's attitudes and acts that produces a more regarding type of school setting. Caring is the chief value in the hierarchy of values and works toward the betterment of the community and the individual person.

Proposals for rendering public schools into caring institutions are not problem free. Beck and Newman's (1993) and Noddings's (1984) caring conception does not demonstrate how to determine personal responsibility when fulfilling general social obligations. This responsibility for a wider public is an obligation that defines an individual's moral-ethical identity, and it underwrites what is meant by ethical rectitude. As Hoagland (1991), following Card (1990), argued, the caring one seems not to have the capacity to consider people in foreign lands in problematic situations of their own making. The caring philosophy has no place for the proximate stranger and hence is incapable of crossing political and social barriers of gender, race, and ethnicity—seen as interests.

Most writers dealing with caring and education seem to overlook the essential contradictions such caring must deal with, both theoretically and practically (Noblit, 1993). Hoagland (1991) correctly detected that "one-caring" has a lack of experience in the world. There is no public in the life of the caring one. Hoagland faulted

Noddings for having limited her attention to local concerns. Hoagland's is a feminist critique, yet it nonetheless speaks for all where she identified the flawed nature of the view: "Caring cannot be insular and it cannot ignore the political reality, material conditions, and social structure of the world" (p. 260).

The most difficult task for any theory of caring is to move from the private to the public moral space. Undifferentiated and abstract caring is a logical trap that comes over us when we accelerate our concern for others to the mass. And it is in the public sphere that principles come into play. Hence the fundamental difficulty facing a theory of caring is to move from individual to plural without sacrificing caring for a principle. Although we can seemingly justify our regard for family or kin, it is not easy to justify caring in general.

Feminists point out the fallacy of characterizing caring as primarily a female instinct. An anthropological study of ethics finds that the source of care in Western society is in the concrete practices of persons within that society, rather than being an innate (gender-specific) attitude. Whether women may possess a type of instinctual predilection to care (for infants for example), the primary impulse has been molded and reshaped by culture such that little of the instinctual survives and what does is impossible to understand without attending to the acculturation process. Humans have evolved biologically to a certain niche point, but the cultural evolution has far more impact on us than we can ever know. We learn to care, not in any overt cognitive way but rather through subtle and not too subtle absorption and refractions of our culture. The repertoire of caring—the many ways in which caring is characterized in our culture—arises in the family, street, and school. Becoming a caring person, adopting a certain set of perceptual considerations in which the body centers the responding being to be open to another, is the result of almost surreal conditioning.

Persons' identities in society as individuals are thus a consequence of bodily learning (as well as logical learning). We have bodily abilities, habits, and arrangements. Parents mold our facial patterns, gestures, voice modulation, and so forth in direct ways. Indirect means are also available for learning to be postured toward the world. Caring must be seen as a fundamental desire and attitude that derives from these sources of control and direction. Nurses and teachers carry themselves in certain ways, and such carriage emanates from the professional codes and rules that surround learned practice. We come to discriminate among individuals by virtue of the ways they present themselves. Among the wide variety of emotional dispositions, caring is imprinted on our body, our organs, nerves, and bones (Fay, 1987).

Political theorists argue that caring is a power relation. Power cavorts as we seek to understand how it works pragmatically. Invariably, power splices our interpersonal relations and colors our communicative efforts. Where nurturing and care become primary, the play of power over the field of transaction is significant. The primary issue here is not school organizational effectiveness but legitimacy. Insofar as we are seeking to impose a liberal and pragmatic test, caring in the context of education must be carried on so that it is nonoppressive and nondominating. Caring conceived of as power calls for legitimate exercise and thus must be freely authorized (Rouse, 1987). We should not be compelled to care but rather come to our caring as free sentient beings.

The current discourse-practice surrounding caring and schooling is set by these historical traditions and informs the sorts of questions and pedagogical procedures we seek to embrace. That educational administration may be in need of a shot in the arm is clear. For decades the field has been moribund, with little innovation discernable in the mainstream organs or institutions that induct leaders into school governance positions. Is caring the nostrum required?

The School as Spiritual Center

The philosophy of compassion and faith entered the discourse of school reform in 19th-century America. With the common school reform movement, religious values were reduced to a nondenominational Protestant ethos. Roman Catholics and other groups were quick to react by seeking to introduce their version of faith into the public school and by building their own schools. In some regions of the United States, the nonpublic schools became elite institutions serving the religious needs of constituents.

Today there is a concern for the nontheological state the public schools have gotten themselves into. Critics point out that public education, in an effort not to offend any particular faith, has turned the school into a spiritual wasteland. Purpel (1989) maintained that teaching and curriculum need to be redesigned in order to introduce once again those difficult "eternal questions." Concern for the nature of the cosmos and humanity must, he argued, yield a common vision of justice, love, community, and joy.

Pragmatism is not free from the potential to link up with a Christian educational mission. Cornel West (1989) fused philosophy and religion into "prophetic pragmatism" (p. 237) by drawing on the historical traditions of both fields. He argued that the contemporary tasks of a responsible and sophisticated philosophy of religion are threefold. The first task is to deepen the historicist turn in philosophy by building on the Quine-Goodman-Sellars contributions and "thickening" the "thin" historicism of Rorty's and Bernstein's neopragmatism by means of undogmatic social analysis and engaged cultural criticism (West, 1993, pp. 130-131). Second, West's pragmatism sets forth moral visions and ethical norms that seek to regulate social analysis and cultural criticism. These ideals are drawn from the best of available religious and secular traditions from the past. Third, his philosophy draws from the world views of various religious and secular traditions, "in light of their comprehensive grasp of the complexity, multiplicity and specificity of human experiences, and their enabling power to motivate human action for the negation and transformation of structures of oppression" (p. 130).

West's prophetic pragmatism confronts existential anguish and social, economic, cultural, and political oppression. As a pragmatist, he has emphasized human experience and moral vision. His is a life-enhancing intellectualism that denies all forms of dogmatism, despair, and oppression. A Left-leaning intellectual, West bows to the influences on his work of Emerson, Marx, and Dewey. He is a postmodern critical pragmatist with his feet in the rich history of intellectual labor yet is deeply committed to relieving the degradation of all peoples. As West (1989) wrote:

> Prophetic pragmatism arrives on the scene as a particular American intervention conscious and critical of its roots, and radically historical and political in its outlook. Furthermore, it gives prominence to the plight of those peoples who

embody and enact the "postmodern" themes of degraded otherness, subjected alienist, and subaltern marginality, that is, the wretched of the earth (poor peoples of color, women, workers). (p. 237)

Schools built on West's prophetic pragmatism would be consciously constructed on historical traditions but would be sensitive to the victims and modes of victimization that have resulted in spiritualless institutions. Steeped in American cultural and intellectual traditions, West's school would become a site of religious revivalism and pragmatic social meliorism.

It is not surprising, given the strong church-state separation views coming from Supreme Court rulings, that there is a marked absence of spiritual values in public schools in America. Americans have always embraced a nonsectarian Protestant value base in public education; however, today a much wider range of religious faiths is represented by students and teachers. The conservative reaction has been to attempt to reintroduce prayer (often slightly disguised Christian prayer at that) into schools. The law is clear that religious sects are not to be allowed to dominate by highlighting their particular religious ideology. On the other hand, it is well within the law to teach about religions, so long as a fuller treatment of the alternatives of faith and belief are set out for the students and so long as one faith is not taught over the others.

Hence, it seems that spirituality may be made part of the school curriculum and daily experiences of students. What the pragmatist holds out for is a wider discussion of faith and belief such that students are informed rather than indoctrinated.

It is important to see the role that faith and hope play in any philosophy of school reform. According to Cornel West (1993), we must be prophetic pragmatists, willing to keep the faith. Rorty (1983, 1989, 1991) has encouraged us to retain hope and to fight against the moral evils that beset our society. And Bernstein (1983) has reinforced any interest in comparison of differing gross frameworks and paradigms to continue the conversation going across differences.

The essential tension, cast in the doctrine of separation of church and state, poses a very real problem for efforts to rebuild American public schools on any religious theme. Recent efforts to include school prayer in public schools have encountered stiff criticism. Are we now ready to admit religious pluralism into an already divisive school setting?

The Aesthetic School

A fourth possibility exists for importing value consideration into schooling: the aesthetic school. Daniel Duke (1986) noted that leadership is not understood by rational analysis but rather arises out of the subjective perception of followers. This subjectivity mirrors the structures of meaning of the perceiver, as well as the culture and times. Thus, for followers to be followers, they must have a commitment to a leader's meaning for the events and relationships within the culture of the organization. By placing things in context, providing purpose and direction, and communicating the values of the organization so a follower's imagination is captured, the leader establishes leadership as an aesthetic enterprise.

It is also possible to speak of education as dedicated to the development of artistic judgment and evaluation (Eisner, 1979/1994). Through a type of "educational connoisseurship" we could come to evaluate school subjects, textbook illustrations, school building architecture, and student performance. Here the attitude and aesthetic sense of the artist would be floated into the normal world of curriculum maker and educational evaluation expert.

However, both Duke and Eisner stop short of casting their lot with an aesthetic school space, a public domain in which all manner of interests interplay. Schools are not much different from the form they took on in the early 1800s; however, culture is vastly different.

Lacking in Duke's and Eisner's characterization is a fuller notion of the aesthetic, a notion that infuses all experiences and spaces with aesthetic quality. In aesthetic critical pragmatism, the apprehension of quality is tightly coupled with the exercise of critical and practical judgment. The latter may be technical, moral-ethical, religious, and so forth, but it is set in motion by the primary condition of quality. Moreover, our efforts as informed school reformers must be to take these primal qualitative features of schooling and move them into the arena of public discourse and debate.

Aesthetic Sense and Schools

Today educational experts read off school problems solutions in the form of engineering and scientific answers. They are without sensitivity to the artistic quality of schools as spaces laced with a variety of values beyond those of rational and technical sorts. Reforms seem to lack the capacity to transcend the language of business and factory because we are blinded to schools being anything else. A new vision of school spaces offering visual, auditory, kinesthetic, and tactile stimulation is required for educational reformers.

Visual

Our language is filled with visual imagery (Ackerman, 1990). We speak of schools in terms of their bulletin boards being "bright splashes of color," the corridors being "dark as tombs," or the grounds being a "barren desert." Yet teacher education and educational administration textbooks are monochromatic, leading us to see the world of the school in shades of gray. Our minds are trained early in our schooling to understand students as products, educational designs as industrial blueprints, and the evaluation of education as equivalent to statistical measures. Courses in art and music are the first to be cut from the schools in economically hard times. Our priority has not been to develop aesthetic judgment in our children and youth. Thus, it is no wonder we find ourselves incapable of either seeing or expressing aesthetic values in terms of school improvement.

Perception is a noncognitive occurrence. When we perceive something, we have an immediate sensory experience of it. We attend to things, but we do so more for what they suggest (in terms of future action) than for what they are in their own right. There is no organ, such as the mind, for cultivating the visual acuity required today. We lack the metaphors and meanings necessary to support such an appendage. The early stages of vision encounter the qualitative, and only later do we engage in logical inference. When we perceive a dark cloud, we take it as a sign that it will rain. We derive from this a symbolic meaning, a meaning of implication. By using language (symbol) we are able to reconstitute a natural sign (cloud) into a significant sign (yielding signification).

Postmodern culture displays new forms of arrangement. Artful in nature, these forms play with traditional elements, realigning them. Scientific inquiry has moved from realism to formalism. Structuralist methods have yielded artificial forms—called schools—only to exclude all other perceptions. The postmodern-poststructural revolution is a revolt in both method (aesthetic vision over scientific logic) and object (school as community space over school as rational organization).

Our experiences come to have influence on us through meaning. Quality plays a part in this meaning attribution. We find a variety of meanings in our experiences; however, when these experiences are of the highest sort, when they cap events—they are aesthetic in nature. Thus, aesthetic quality is found in art, but it is also found in thinking as well.

In terms of schools and school reform, it is evident that the meanings derived from experiences within educational organizations fall into three categories: (a) intrinsic meaning, or the meaning intrinsic to natural events as experienced immediately or "had experiences"; (b) sign-significance meaning, or the relation of inference, or significance; in other words, extrinsic or instrumental meaning as the meaning that moves us from raw experience to intelligent understanding relative to some end-in-view; and (c) symbolic meaning, or meaning as used in linguistic operations for developing the implications of experience, a type of logical meaning. Little emphasis is placed on meanings for experiences that a person has "had." Typically, we spend most of our time dealing with meanings of the last two types.

School reformers must begin to pay attention to intrinsic value experience. When Bill Gates of Microsoft Corporation began purchasing rights to duplicate entire art museums for his software business, he must have believed that works of art would play a big role in our educational programs in the future.

Auditory

We pay very little attention to the sounds of experience. Schools are constructed to control and dampen noise. Yet it is through sound that children communicate, teachers teach, and administrators lead.

Music is essentially a language, as important as one's native tongue. Music is the basis for mathematics. Public speaking and rhetoric are no longer emphasized in classrooms, yet in the political arena the demand for such skills is evident.

When budgets become tight, one of the first programs to feel cuts is the music program. Band instruments and choir trips are expensive, and they do not lead to improved test scores on the ACT or the SAT. The debate team and the speech club are also subject to cavalier treatment. We cannot seem to justify these experiences for children; yet they make us fuller citizens and human beings.

On the horizon of innovation is distance education. Through computer-telephone technology it is possible to deliver school subjects at great distances. The cyberspace of Internet provides yet another auditory and visual means of moving students into the postmodern future. The crucial question is whether the school will incorporate the aesthetic side of this technological revolution.

Kinesthetic

Fesmire (1994) has said that moral artistry is expressed in the dramatic rehearsal of options for solving the problems we face. Thus critical intelligence is aesthetic if we try on alternative visions of the future as solutions to our difficulty. This rehearsal gains a moral bite on experience where the experience becomes emotional; it becomes scientific where it takes on a rational cast. The individual choice is rehearsed through dramatic play acting. The intended course of action is mentally rehearsed and the bodily gestures are tried out.

The rhythm of human experience is the cadence invoked by struggle and resistance. This refusal to accept an experience as unresolved occurs when encountering a problem or difficulty. If the problem is worked on intelligently, a consummatory experience may result. Critical pragmatism finds resistance to be primarily a freeing of dominated experience. One trend is to locate schools within warehouses or other vacant spaces. These types of buildings provide excellent facilities for dance, music, and other sorts of kinesthetic activities.

Tactile

Another aesthetic channel is tactile in nature. Children learn from touching things—the rough texture of sandpaper, the smoothness of glass. These surfaces teach the meanings of words and concepts. One of the cruelest diseases is Hansen's disease (once called leprosy) because its victims are gradually denied the sense of touch.

Schools are not experimental spaces for the cultivation of the sense of touch, nor do we find architects to be as sensitive as sculptors to the importance of feeling the edges and surfaces of their creations. The blind develop their sense of touch to compensate for the loss of sight, but the sighted seem strangely uncomfortable with the feel of things. Schools must be redirected toward being centers of tactile learning relative to people and things. Dewey and the progressive educators told us that children "learn by doing." A sense of touch is cultivated in schools in which activities are foremost.

Artistry

In an epilogue, Bolman and Deal (1991) have moved away from the static serial frameworks to a larger perspective. Educational organization looked at from multiframes—as machine, family, jungle, and theater—"requires the capacity to think in different ways at the same time about the same thing" (p. 450).

> Without wise leaders and artistic managers to help close the gap, we will continue to see misdirected resources, massive ineffectiveness, and unnecessary pain and suffering. . . . We see prodigious challenges for organizations in the future and for those who will guide them, yet we are still optimistic. We hope . . . [their efforts] will lay the groundwork for a new generation of managers and leaders who recognize the importance of poetry and philosophy, as well as analysis and technique, and who embrace the fundamental values of human life and the human spirit. (Bolman & Deal, 1991, pp. 450-451)

Following Bolman and Deal (1991), it may be said that an aesthetic approach is just another framework, but this is incorrect. Frameworks have been formal devices, but aesthetics looks behind these frames. It looks at all such intellectual framings as artificial. Once constructed, they engage in self-perpetuation and reification. Framed concepts and webs take on a life of their own, and we debate their meanings in endless rounds of academic conferences.

Through the means of artistic creativity, it is possible to view our institutions and render their chaos into order, to attend to quality rather than mere realignment and reconfiguration of quantity. However, unlike the portrait painted by Deal and Peterson (1994) of a forced choice between polar opposite leadership styles, logical versus artistic, we must see the artistic preliminary encounter with experiential quality. Only later is logic affixed to these experiences.

Aesthetic Tools

Design

John Dewey (1934) noted that the word *design* has a double meaning. It stands for a purpose, and it signifies an arrangement. The design of a school is the plan for that school; it is also the arrangement of the elements of the school (classrooms, cafeteria, auditorium, gymnasium, etc.). A good design—for a school or anything else—is valuable when the parts contribute to the consummation of a conscious experience. A good design takes on and provides form.

During the colonial period in America, school could be kept in any type of building. In the first half of the 19th century, the Lancastrian schools were popular. Large numbers of students (as many as 300) were instructed in one lecture hall. Older pupils called "monitors" instructed younger ones. After 1834 the Prussian system of the common school reformers introduced the idea of separate classrooms for different age groups. Henry Barnard, a follower of Horace Mann, fought for a new school architecture that conceived of the school as a Greek temple. The use of columns and large steps to a central entrance became popular in the wake of the Greek revival.

With the large increases in pupil numbers, schools gradually came to resemble factories until the early 1900s, when progressive educators exercised their influence. According to these reformers, children learned best when allowed to pursue their own natural interests. John Dewey's (1899/1915) famous booklet *School and Society* stressed the need for work tables and chairs for activities to replace stationary desks designed for listening.

The heyday for school architects was during the decades of the 1950s, 1960s, and 1970s. Federal money lubricated the coffers of design firms. From the great number of plans emerged the open-spaced school and the open-classroom plans. Critics argued that open education was often foisted on unwilling educators, that teachers were rarely prepared to teach within this open context, and that noise and distractions made teaching and learning difficult.

In the 1970s and 1980s the reaction to open education resulted in a type of eclectic design and a retreat "back to basics." Schools built during these years found allegiance to openness in the form of group spaces. However, students were attached to homerooms and required a place to store personal possessions (Ahrentzen, 1988). Eclecticism erupted in regionalism, in which schools came to resemble neocolonial barns and stables, prairie villages, or warehouse lofts. Back to basics in curriculum and teaching resulted in a return to modular box construction with an industrial look.

However, with the restructuring reforms have come calls for new school designs to match the philosophy. Around the country school administrators, board members, and others are exploring ways to break the mold of the 1950s architecture and to create school facilities that reflect new organizational concepts. Decentering of control will have to be translated into decentered spaces, clustering will have to be transferred to multiclassroom pods, and the romance of smaller schools will need to be carried into more tightly connected classrooms (Gunts, 1993).

Government will certainly become involved in new school designs as parents express concern for the dangers posed to their children from outside. Just as schools have been made more accessible to disabled students following the passage of federal legislation, so the entrances, water fountains, corridors, and so forth will be reconfigured for greater accessibility to all participants. New design teams made up of architects, clients, children, child psychologists, and so on are needed. These experts will form a multidisciplinary approach to the design of schools on the basis of the users—children—and their development. Because the child's cognitive, social, emotional, and physical development are shaped in part by the environment, all the senses will have to be engaged by the designed spaces.

Current trends in school design express ideas such as community center schools, regional and climate-sensitive schools, schools for flexible teaching methods, technologically equipped classrooms, schools that may swell or shrink based on enrollments, and multipurpose schools.

Educational reform movements will be an important stimulus for future school design projects, providing steady work for many architects, as school leaders launch a new wave of school additions, alterations, and fresh building. Design must be made to serve children: Make-do designs are no longer acceptable (Gunts, 1993).

Playfulness

Eisner (1979/1994) pointed out that play opens up new possibilities in teaching as a form of artistry. Teachers as artists using play are able to exploit new options as they occur and are less dedicated to the rules of the game. Aims and the structures of schools become more fluid and open. Leadership becomes less linear and technical. As Bolman and Deal (1991) related, leaders and managers will be

> playful theorists who can see organizations through a complex prism. They will be negotiators able to design elastic strategies that simultaneously shape events and adapt to changing circumstances. They will understand the importance of knowing and caring for themselves and those with whom they work. They will, in short, be architects, catalysts, advocates, prophets, and poets. (p. 451)

Intelligence comes into play when we use deliberation to rehearse or envision possible or probable courses of action that may be taken in solving a problem. Such courses of action are aimed at integrating competing desires that have issued in disequilibrium or chaos and that seek to restore equilibrium and harmony.

Aesthetic Meliorism

Reforming education requires intercession. The organization of the school and the reigning theories that make sense of that organizational life auger against such reform. We must engage in a meliorism or active involvement in the reconstruction of experiences.

A tandem difficulty was posed by Dewey regarding how to make art transactional with society. Historically, we find a sharp dividing line between the workaday world of capital accumulation and the "museum" notion of art. Dewey believed that a reunification of art and life was needed. Schools can become places of artful intercession, spaces in which aesthetics may be used as tools of creation and appraisal.

Valuation and School Reconstruction

I have traced several proposals for seeing ethical, moral, spiritual, and aesthetic values in schools. The problems facing school administration and management in a reconstructed educational setting and the weaknesses of some of these approaches have been revealed. Now, if we are not content to embrace these theories of school restructure, what is left? There are at least three alternatives: (a) We may abandon all talk of values relative to school organization; (b) we may select some other theory of values and apply it to school redesign; or (c) we may rethink the role of aesthetic, moral, and ethical values and school organization.

If we abandon talk of values of a moral and ethical type in considering school patterns, we fall prey to an earlier error in moral-ethical theorizing, an error particularly prevalent in American society. Historically, those thinkers who were impatient with the lack of empirically testable indicators of morals or ethics felt that the whole language was merely a set of emotive responses. Because there was no way to scientifically validate moral or ethical pronouncements, they were pushed out of the picture and emphasis was placed on scientific pronouncements. Value (moral or ethical) assertions relative to school restructure, given the emotivist position, are simply nonsense.

A second theoretical effect of taking ethics and morals in a particular way is to interpret school redesign relative to some moral-ethical perspective. Ethics based on caring seeks to reject an ethics built either on principles or on utility. These two perspectives have been popular for centuries, the first embraced by Kant and the second by the British utilitarians. The force of taking a principles or utility perspective is to move the consideration of value matters to a type of rational calculus applied in a post hoc or rarefied hypothetical manner.

A third approach is necessary, one that calls for us to rethink the role of values of all sorts (moral, ethical, religious, aesthetic, etc.) in judgments having to do with school organization. A pragmatic naturalistic finds that school organization has a moral purpose. Having said this, we must also admit that there is nothing inherent in the plan of restructure that makes a reformed school moral. The idea of school redesign does not itself possess moral or immoral properties; rather, it is how the idea influences the patterned outcomes that makes it moral or immoral (or amoral). In simple language, the value (moral or ethical in this case) emerges in the connections that link an idea to its consequences, such that the design has value meaning for the persons who work and learn in the school.

Arguing from the standpoint that a moral-ethical school design is located in some set of external principles or universal notions of value is to miss the vast differences such principles mirror in real situations. Arguing from the perspective that a moral-ethical school design is a matter of the greatest good for the greatest number faces the problem of failing to come to the aid of the disenfranchised and silent minorities. In both instances there is nothing to dictate moral or ethical behavior in the ideas themselves.

As Dewey (1909) noted, needed is some way for such moral-ethical ideas to become "moving ideas" that motivate conduct (p. 3). All schooling has a moral purpose in the sense that it aims at enlarging the capacity of children and youth to master the subject matters and intellectual moves in order that they can render their behavior more vigorous, consistent, and fruitful than otherwise.

Schools are social institutions, and their moral responsibility is to society (Dewey, 1909). The structure and organization of schools must be rethought in terms of this social responsibility. Unfortunately, the tendency has been to set sights on the citizenship preparation aim of schooling as the single indicator of this responsibility. However, as Dewey noted, there is more to it than this. Schools must be so patterned and ordered as to promote children becoming workers, family members, and so forth. And schools themselves are seen as miniature societies in their own right. The moral role here is significant.

It is important to note that the critical pragmatist values may be talked of in two distinct ways. First, value resides in the experiences we have in the form of prizing, cherishing, and treasuring. In this sense the value of an experience is had. A second meaning of value is evaluating. Here we introduce judgment to the valuing process. For Dewey, we may use scientific methods in the latter range of valuing. For other pragmatists, we may employ literary analysis and phenomenological techniques.

Through the application of methods of practical judgment to the problems of school organization, it is possible to determine courses of future structure that enhance the good-making character of the institution and society. Valued arrangements of education are not simply empirical properties. We cannot simply inquire into present educational arrangements and find the best future arrangements. An evaluation process is needed to render these values appropriate for the postmodern society.

We must locate our method of valuation in a naturalist view. All nature is made up of transactions, some of which have their own qualitative ends. These endings are the resources of values we may draw on for our plans and policies. Humans are involved in such natural transactions, making them more complex and at times chaotic. Where there are conflicts over immediate values (desirables) a choice must be made. The process of inquiry is necessary and we come to form new ends-in-view to resolve the conflicts. A joining of the prizing and the appraisal functions becomes evident.

As we scrutinize plans for school redesign, it is important to find ends that are artful consummatory experiences. Our outcomes should be marked by completeness and integrity rather than mere effectiveness. One of the problems with contemporary school reorganization movements is that reformers overlook the need for this consummatory character of school life: It must be good. We as a nation shy away from talking of the good school in this larger sense.

Where we consider organized forms of school life, we thus have patterns and parts of patterns of education that we prize and hold dear. These aspects of school structure we may regard as having merit. On the other hand, we may inquire into the aspects of the school organization in a critical and judgmental way, attempting to test out for future experience the worth of the structured experiences (both had and contemplated) and interactions we have located. This second aspect of valuing is significant as it provides *normative* recommendations as to how school must be reordered relative to certain norms or standards we hold acceptable. Previous chapters have shown how important such practical judging is.

It is essential to grasp the fact that values that enter into the judgment (valuation) of patterned schooling are *transformed* as they become connected with the aims of schools. We begin with prized features of school life; evaluate these in terms of the problems, conflicts, and chaos of the situation; employ intelligent procedures; and choose the appropriate alternative for their resolution. As we move through this process, both the so-called original valuables and the outcomes become changed and redirected. Nothing really stays the same.

Having said all of this, it is significant to realize that naturalized ethics and morals as appropriated for school redesign must deal with schools as collective and patterned social responses to the demands of societies. One significant feature of this responsibility is the role *continuity* plays in the life of any social institution. Schools as institutions tend to be conservative social devices, resistant to change. The continuity of forms of educational governance, subject matter, and teaching methods is obvious, but beyond these forms are the regularities and uniformities regarding the status of the institution as a school and its place in society. On the latter ground, nothing radically different has emerged in nearly 200 years.

Further, as Bernstein (1966) pointed out, pragmatists are vague on the means to be employed to sort out those continuities that are worthwhile versus those that are not. How are we to judge which continuous forms of school organization are worth preserving? An answer is available to us. Unfortunately, recent chaos writings introduce inadequate dichotomies and breaks in experience, and they provide explanatory means for their rectification. We are told chaos is everywhere in our institutions and organizations. The means to address this state of affairs is to employ chaos theory. Measurement methods are said to explain its dynamics. Chaos theorists propose that what initially appeared as disorder is now a deeper and more sublime order. The effect of such reasoning is to move the lens of explanation from the general (chaos) to the particular (order) and then explain the chaos whole as a piece of the particular. The logic of such argument is suspicious. How can the part explain the whole except by becoming another whole at a different level?

Constructing the New School Order

In the last analysis, schools as centers of educative life must find inhabitants engaged in aesthetic and experimental behaviors. Inquiry is nothing if it is not engaged in reconstruction of the space we have taken to be given. Through socially proactive inquiry we may avoid the trap of blaming the victims and shirking our responsibility to reconstruct the moral norms used in our judgments. Postmodern pragmatic philosophy is done with an eye to boundaries that form local arenas of interest, contingent rather than absolute in nature.

Postmodernists warn of the debacle and the collapse of rationality. There is a jettisoning of metanarratives (and metavalues) to underwrite our actions. Postmodernist Baudrillard (1993) has pointed to modernist simulations of events and characters. We have lost a grip on what is real. In a mad scramble we seek to latch on to elusive images of who we are and what our existence means. Schools as organizations operate as simulations of the real. Artificial linguistic characterizations purify the hardscrabble lives lived in schools.

Narratives, icons, and rituals are silenced, overlooked, and ignored; as a consequence, all that we treasure as education falls about our ears.

However, because Rorty (1989) found our institutions dominated by such rigid and anterior norms and discourses, he argued that we must locate a playing field on which ideas are examined or considered and radical ironies explored. A social space is needed in which individuals in communities engage in moral decisions such as to constitute a school as a moral democracy. Power (1993) noted that such a moral school atmosphere would be an effective counter to the radical individualism so pronounced in American society today. Had we heeded the words of John Dewey (1916a), we might have avoided the undisciplined, crime-ridden, meandering institution the school has become. Dewey had early cautioned that schools as institutions had become overly rigid and formal. Children were viewed as passive and immature organisms awaiting imposition of subject matter. Teachers were taken as workers who required stern management. For Dewey the school was a microcosm of the larger society but ideal in nature because it served as a testing ground for improved arrangements. The school itself served as the moral-ethical instrument of sociocultural reconstruction. It was impossible for the school to eliminate the existing evils of society if it did not constitute a social environment of the most sublime moral-ethical type. The school was seen as the social instrument, utilizing open methods of inquiry and problem solving, manifesting individual students possessing the required moral-ethical character and intelligence to operate on this character such that the society at large could be improved in terms of aesthetic quality. We have forgotten or ignored Dewey's philosophy to our detriment.

The notion that schools can be so designed seems to have escaped the school restructuring movement. The school culture and environment are powerful determinants in educational success. When the school is arranged to enhance the virtues of trust, integrity, courage, and so forth, there is a moral-ethical pattern of interactions. Where such experiences are continuous and repetitive, we have a moral-ethical community of harmony and beauty.

Previous chapters have noted that we face complex problems in the schools and that only by intelligent judgments applied to such disorder may we work our way out of the confusion of the present era. Democracy in the schools has been proposed as the best social and political arrangement to foster such decision making. Decisions are the heart of ethical and moral thought and action. Hence, we begin with the raw qualities of experience and then adopt intelligence to the aesthetic ideal of democracy. The fruits of such a school redesign are awesome to contemplate because they would determine a new, more moral America.

If we think of the moral school as an artist's studio, we are able to use pragmatic metaphors to better approximate a revolution in thinking about the organization and function of schools. Take, for example, the school as a weaver's studio in which the artist-educator comes to inquire into and understand competing values—people's desires, needs, and goals—as threads of experience that must be interwoven into a tapestry of meaning. The educator qua artist is able to take the point of view of others with their interests and desires and to seek a harmonious whole—a moral ideal space within which competing interests become harmonious (Fesmire, 1994).

When we propose a conception of schooling as an ideal democratic arrangement, it becomes a form of life that has a moral component. We must look at this moral ideal from a number of perspectives, one of which is aesthetic. Democratically arranged spaces may be characterized using scientific, political, economic, or some other language and notions, but I believe we are long overdue in looking at schools as democratically arranged spaces with aesthetic features.

School governance has historically dealt with the internal operations of the school as well as the relation the school has with the community. The key players have been the superintendent, principal, and their assistants. Presently, there is little agreement as to the responsibilities of these administrators, particularly the assistant principal (Marshall, 1992). Schools may be organized for either freedom or autocracy relative to their roles. We are leaving a historical era that prized autocratic and bureaucratic devices for delivering the social purpose of education. We are embarking on school reforms that treasure the value of freedom—for teachers, students, parents, and community members—in framing the purposes for which schools shall be organized.

The directives for such a model of school redesign pledged to the value of freedom are several. We must see school administration as a field of study undertaking a critical self-reflection in which the privileged theories of autocratic school leadership are jettisoned. Dialogue regarding the purpose of schooling should move from narrow notions of effectiveness and efficiency to larger arenas of valued outcome. We must see that in all eras, school administration has been and will be a form of politics. Administration must take into consideration the culture at large and the school culture. School administration must be based on democracy and democratic decision making. Administrative leaderships must be committed to encouraging leadership among all individuals involved in the school.

One of the supreme problems for pragmatic critics of caring and other desire theories of ethics is to move from individual self-interest to the social interest. Habermas (1993) has warned that a mere pragmatic interest in solving each new problem according to a new logic of practical judgment is incoherent. He found the good and the just slighted in this emphasis on the purposive dimension of ethical judgment. How may we bring persons to see the essential part they must play in the larger community? The key part in this puzzle is the role played by integrity. Where the individual in the democracy may fulfill her or his individual potential, an integration of character occurs in which strength is built via choosing. The more connected we are with the resources of the organization and the more we are a part of the decisions as to how these are brought to bear on the educational activities of the school, the more we build integrity. The more we play a part in organizing and deciding educational acts, the more likely will moral-ethical character be created and reinforced. Pragmatist William H. Kilpatrick found that character was created by choice making (Childs, 1956). Older patterns of school organization cut off the teachers, parents, and students from choices, with the result that their characters were built in partial and truncated fashion. Many of our modern problems attached to schools (discipline, drugs, violence, etc.) may be explained from this standpoint.

Democracy has been advanced as a platform from which to work toward school reorder. By embracing democracy as a social ethic, we secure the mechanism by which schools as social institutions form and re-form into patterned forms of life. There is an organic nature to this construction and reconstruction that should not be overlooked. The naturalism espoused by critical pragmatism provides an element of faith in the aesthetic, ethical, moral power of humans to create sound means for fulfilling their desires. Students in schools are guided by teachers in the processes necessary for inquiring into the problems they and the community face. The democratic nature of the setting and impulse provokes the search for better alternatives. Without democracy, we have chaos.

School redesign is a value activity as we engage in artistic processes of creation. New forms of schooling are needed as we face the challenges of the 21st century. No ready-made answers are provided. The artistic impulse provides a way of communicating aesthetic images of the desired patterns of institutional life. Aesthetic values and artistic valuation are no less significant than ethics and morals. Each provides a dimension of the process and influences the completeness of the outcome.

The design is both an idea and an outcome. Schools are not static flowcharts or ledger sheets. Art helps to intensify ordinary experience through patterned arrangements. The shaping of school experiences is done through the forms applied to teaching, administering, counseling, coaching, and so forth. The form of school life is the manner in which the parts of the school process are arranged, sequenced, and interrelated. Some of these parts of the arrangement are tightly coupled and some are loosely coupled. The successful school is so patterned that it enhances the development of students. Form provides continuity to the arrangement of the school, allowing it to develop and grow. Equilibrium comes from tension. The form of organization is reached when a stable but flowing equilibrium is reached. Chaos is controlled and made orderly.

The shift from one form of organization to another is time based, necessitates involvement, and emanates from some problematic status. The current school as an organization is indeterminate and is failing to achieve its moral responsibilities to the individuals, community, and society it is designed to serve. Today, school reforms that tout decentralization, site-based management, and local decision making are efforts to intelligently and creatively reconfigure the system by which teaching-learning moves the immature of our society toward maturity. The fact that extraneous factors inhibit this growth is all the more frustrating because many of these factors are beyond the control of the school (family breakups, crime, drugs, etc.). Where the values that cut through the school operation are detrimental to the mission of the school, new ones need to be introduced. This issuing of new norms and standards is a matter of appraisal and has the blessing of democracy seen as judgmental and practical process because the richness of the outcomes is tested in terms of the moving ideas we embrace as we rebuild our school institutions. The fruits of such reforms are tested in the day-to-day ways in which students come to be participants in our communities and society.

Schools as Social Spaces

We oversimplify schools. We forget that they are spaces, social spaces in the case of public schools, in which a variety of interests play for attention. Life in school is a continuous transaction between persons and that space. At times these transactions are marked by chaos or disequilibrium, at other times order and equilibrium. When a child, teacher, or administrator falls out of step with these surroundings and then recovers harmony with them, we see evidence of growth. As Dewey (1934) put it: "Life grows when a temporary falling out is a transition to a more extensive balance of the energies of the organism with those of the conditions under which it lives" (pp. 19-20). However, such growth is not just quantitative but also qualitative in nature. The person moves to a more significant and higher powered level of existence. We find a restored harmony and what Rorty (1985) called "solidarity" with the space occupied (p. 16).

Certainly one difficulty in trying to speak of the aesthetic quality of schools as spaces is found in the barriers encountered with allied efforts to discuss the school and its culture and climate. Following Cusick (1987), Hoy and Miskel (1991) noted: "Although organizational culture has become a fashionable construct for analysis in education, much of the recent discussion of school culture remains analytical, philosophical, and rhetorical rather than empirical" (p. 218). Hoy and Miskel then slip naturally into a discussion of "effective school cultures" yet admit there are few "thick descriptions of qualitative studies to map the basic assumptions and common values of the cultures of schools" (p. 218). One exemplary effort appears to be the work of Firestone and Wilson (1985) on cultural content and symbols, and "primary communication patterns" (Hoy & Miskel, 1991, p. 219). Three symbol systems are identified: *stories*, or narratives, myths, and tales; *icons*, or physical artifacts (e.g., trophies, mottos, logos); and *rituals*, or ceremonies (assemblies, graduation exercises, etc.). By examining how these symbols work their way into life, Hoy and Miskel found it possible to test out organizational effectiveness once again.

Bates (1987) has been cited as a critic of organizational culture research. After Hoy and Miskel committed the error of identifying organizational culture with what managers wish to see there, they pointed to Bates, who asserted that what is good for management is not necessarily good for workers. Hoy and Miskel demonstrated in their own narrative of this research theme, and Bates also identified in such studies that the effort to firm up inquiry into school culture by calling for empirical indicators and then castigating such studies for failing to show how effectiveness may be enhanced is to revert to a structuralist and modernist research framework and set of biases that fail to be sensitive to the aesthetic qualities of school spaces. It seems we are able to reach the edge of the pool but lack the courage to plunge in!

Educational Appraisal

The qualities that reside within the space of school are not always apparent. Hence we need something such as Eisner's (1979/1994) connoisseurship to unearth them. Nor are they recognized as worthwhile or supported by persons within or outside the complex of the school, once they are brought to our attention. This is where democracy comes in. In a democratic space, the competing qualities are given maximal opportunity to surface and be scrutinized for encapsulation into the normative life of the institution.

Mostly we are without vision regarding where schools and students ought to be going; our eyes are not sensitized nor is our knowledge sufficient to see. We must educate the eye, the hand, and the ear early in a child's life.

If we were to experience a reconstructive effort relative to schools, it would be possible to bring to bear on the effort a critical and pragmatic perspective—one that situates the discourse of policy and policy formation within a new postliberal arena, with the aim of designing a center to match the educational directions taken in a postmodern culture. What would a postmodern school look like if it matched the demands of moral-ethical concern? Given a type of democracy that is postliberal in nature and the anticipated postmodern nature of cultural development in the coming decades, it is possible to specify a prototype school pivoting on participation. The school should be a social space within which a variety of voices, icons, and rituals resonate; critical intelligence and pragmatic acumen flourish; and children and youth engage in the artful reconstruction of experience with an eye to enrichment and growth.

At the heart of this call for a new type of school is the urge to embrace the postmodern over the modern, the postliberal over the liberal—a pragmatic temper that is at once reflective and aesthetic-moral-ethical in its interests. The fundamental feature of pragmatism is the emphasis placed on tests and consequences rather than airy debate and artificial studies. The academic social scientist must be joined with the concerned citizen in order that participation within the public space called school becomes valued over rational-technical expertise.

In short, schools must be transformed into postmodern social spaces in which aesthetic discourse may be jointly engaged in relative to the question, "How ought we to create a new school order?" At the heart of my recommendation is a commitment to the belief that all school participants may enter into collaborative inquiry and participate in an aesthetic, moral, ethical dialogue in a host community pledged to postliberal and democratic norms of intelligent educational reconstruction.

John Dewey said it best in his book *Art as Experience* (1934):

> We live in a world in which there is an immense amount of organization, but it is an external organization, not one of the ordering of a growing experience, one that involves, moreover, the whole of the live creature, toward a fulfilling conclusion. . . . The remaking of the material of experience in the act of expression is not an isolated event confined to the artist and to a person here and there who happens to

enjoy the work. In the degree in which art exercises its office, it is also a remaking of the experience of the community in the direction of greater order and unity. (p. 81)

Conclusions

The school must be reexamined with the eye of an artist. For too long we have evaluated educational processes and products and found these ineffective or unproductive. By recasting the school as a social space, attaching to it a democratic ideal, and casting ourselves in the part of moral artists, we may reconstruct educational sites into beautiful places for helping children to grow into ethical, moral, and aesthetic democratic citizens.

7

Conclusions

American public education and culture suffer from the consequences of two countervailing forces. On the one hand, we are facing a fragmentation, pluralization, and decentering of public life and institutions of an extraordinary intensity. Efforts to break away from the mainstream and form cults and enclaves of difference pervade schools and society. A radical individualism dominates our American impulse at the present time and with it are the anomie and alienation that support distinctness.

In the face of the breakdown in the social cohesiveness and school uniformity, there are a number of counters. First, there is the effort of community theorists to resurrect communal forms. In the political sphere, the thrust takes the form of small community groups, town-meeting type formats, and local groups. The argument is that just as in our historical past, when the New England town formed the nexus of American life, so today we may reconstitute such small, face-to-face communities in the city, in the workplace, and in the school to offset the evils of modernity and faceless bureaucracy.

A second counter is put forward by multiculturalists, who argue that America is a plurality of culture groups. The American democracy is a competing set of racial, ethnic, and other interests that seek dominance. Only through the free interplay of such interests does the public get served. Organizations are arrangements of such interests and provide a playing field on which such groups compete for attention and control. For some, multicultural interest group pluralism is attached to democratic theory.

A third counter to the rigidity of American social institutions and American culture is that of a critical and pragmatic reconstruction. With this approach (the one favored in this text), individual human beings come together because of similar interests and form patterned responses to the problems they face. Through the use of aesthetic regard and discussion, persons participate in dialogue over the merits of alternative policies for correcting the ills they face.

Emancipatory in nature, this third postmodern, democratic cultural pluralism view finds some organizations and pieces of organizations to be debilitating and disqualifying of participation. The postmodern notion of patterned life comes to the rescue as it highlights the features of organizations in modernist culture and offers methodological correctives. Attached to the postmodern view of schools as forms is the notion that crucial changes are needed in how we perceive such social spaces. Postmodernists offer a variety of tools, dialogue, aesthetic moral intelligence, and community building for rethinking organizational theory. However, it is important to understand that these postmodern tools are merely instruments for emancipating our viewpoint and not ends in themselves. Thus postmodernity strives to avoid the casting of itself into a framework or some metanarrative.

Throughout this text the importance of a critical pragmatism to the future of schooling has been stressed. I have proposed that the pragmatism of John Dewey provides a route to uncovering the linkage between human experience, pluralistic and communal in nature, and the problems of contemporary postmodern socioculture. Needed is a complete rethinking of the intelligent basis for understanding the nature and place of schools within society. Through the means of an aesthetic and critical intelligence, I believe that we can analyze and locate the appropriate middle-range moves that will pattern the changes necessary. An emphasis on democracy as the mode of postmodern arrangements for social life leads us toward a cultural diversity that reveals marginalized groups and silenced voices, elevates dialogue and conversation to the level of transactional discourse-practice, and moves us toward a leadership of a collective and informed sort aimed at coherence and continuity.

Suggestions for School Reconstruction

Frameworks. The first piece of advice for school reformers is to avoid the frameworks trap. Frameworks thinking leads to entrapment in relativism or objectivism. A moral artistry dedicated to a pragmatic interest in critical and intellectual processes is needed.

Chaos versus order. In the mid-1980s Frederick Crews (1986) rightly noted something of a reunification of the two cultures of C. P. Snow—the sciences and the arts—was under way. In the 1950s and 1960s scientists rejected the fuzzy world of ideas in their hard scramble to acquire facts. Positivism in its many guises dominated the laboratories. This all has changed in the last decade: Recently science and philosophy have joined hands in attempting to provide fuller explanations of the phenomena they view. Chaos theory, in its many forms, is one such effort to bridge the gap between the two cultures.

The present text warns against adopting the view that all is chaotic in schools and culture. There is evidence for both chaos and order. The function of human intelligence is to make sense out of the world. I caution school redesigners to recognize extant complexity while seeking to simplify and reconstitute the essential ingredients in schooling. Smaller scale institutions may work in some situations, larger ones in others. Following John Dewey, it is important that the process of dealing with chaos and complexity is continuous reconstruction of experience in order to gain greater control over future experience. Educational reconstruction must be open to the variety of values of culture and seek to encapsulate these in school spaces.

Democracy and educational organization. Democracy as a method of practical deliberation and for the exercise of choice has been supported in the face of school restructuring efforts. Snauwaert (1993) argued that, although school-based management as part of educational reform today is a significant move toward democracy, it contains two flaws: Current reforms favor either professionalism or community empowerment, thus weakening the outcome; and reforms that retain control in traditional bureaucrats at state, district, or local levels tend to encourage accountability and efficiency over true empowerment of teachers, parents, and students of local schools. The solution is "developmental democracy," in which teachers as educational professionals are empowered as are parents and citizens. Equal decision-making power is extended to both groups in Snauwaert's model, and collaborative collective judgments are the goal. In like manner the local school committee must see itself sharing power with the traditional governance structures of education. The result is a compound structure with overlaps of power and jurisdiction.

Snauwaert (1993) proposes a democracy based on choice. He believes that we have premised this freedom of choice on the value of efficiency rather than human development. We should adopt a democratic system that encourages schools built on principles of participation, communication, association, nonviolence, and community. Although these underlying values could provoke a variety of systemic outcomes, Snauwaert proposes one. He sees this version of democracy enabling a compound structure, with direct participation in decision making, combined forms of representation, consensual decision making based on dialogue, transformational leadership, political education and organization, due process, and juridical standards.

The envisioned plan provides a bottom-up design with direct participation in deliberations. Such a vehicle would maximize individual human development, as Snauwaert (1993) suggests. Schools with such a system of school governance would not ensure success. Other variables such as funding, technology, teachers, and staff would affect educational excellence. However, where the system is democratized, a genuine representation of all parties could occur, "possibly leading to a change in school finance" (p. 104).

I am inclined to propose democracy as a moral ideal providing a means for the individual to realize her or his personal potential while adding to the community's merits. There is a need for a set of assumptions that fuel such an organized way of life. A democracy resting on a critical pragmatic approach is superior to one that simply favors participation in decision making. There are evils in the world, and only through critical dialogue can these be identified and remedied. Of course, this critique assumes that we share and collaborate in our inquiry, that we exercise judgmental skill, and that we honestly test the concrete consequences of our plans.

School restructuring is failing, not because it is inefficient or lacks proper means for accounting for "school effects"; the problem is deeper than this. We must refocus and turn away from modernist assumptions regarding the way organizations and persons flourish. Postmodern schools as new forms of educational space should be built on the twin values of democracy and educational value. The ways in which schools will be redesigned and the attitudes students, parents, teachers, and administrators take toward them will be quite different. The educational merit of school will be determined in new ways. The pedagogy will manifest itself in new modes. Administration will become transactional leadership.

Postmodernism and leadership. It is vital to seek in schooling for the next century a sensitivity to place and a respect for change. We must rethink the simplistic cultural models of previous reforms. An affirmative rather than skeptical version of postmodernism is needed. Rather than being viewed as a chaos of nihilism and alienation, the new postmodern culture must be seen as one of assurance and strength. Leadership of a transactional nature is stressed as the meliorative device for transforming culture and bringing about a new, more humane social order.

Cultural diversity. Although American culture may be pluralistic in fact, we must realize that any efforts to restructure schools for that diversity will be human efforts with virtues and pitfalls. We cannot simply import the diverse features of American society into the schools: Our task is one of selection and appropriation of cultural meanings.

We have seen how one group, Hispanics, may come to play a greater part in the mosaic of American cultural pluralism. The virtues of Hispanic education and leadership toward the end of a more solidified and affirmative self-image are a function of Hispanic leadership.

Moral artistry for a new school order. In the face of contemporary calls for school restructuring, it is vital to stress the necessity of developing aesthetic, moral, and ethical stances toward schools. The increasingly fragmented nature of American culture is a function of conscious and subconscious efforts to link separateness to skin color, folklore, and sexuality. Without denying the import of such considerations, school redesign is shortsighted where it fails to locate the engine of individual and social growth in factors that divide without lifting up the divided ones. By focusing on art as moral-ethical in our approach to life's plurality, we hope to see a life of artful composition, rather than one of divisive decomposition, chaos, and breakdown.

A Final Word

In summary, school reform will work best when it draws on a democratic social ideal, seeks to provide an artistic-intellectual (practical judgment) approach to the problems of conflict and competition among individuals and interests, and works toward a meliorative duty to the continuity and sustenance of the school. We must continue to hold out hope for new forms and patterns of schooling that will help us marshal the potential of postmodern culture while keeping an eye on the resident values of coherence and continuity.

The critical pragmatism offered here is seen as a process for the transformation of our modernist culture into a postmodern culture that energizes the power of each and every one of us to make our schools and society rich with democratic possibilities. Schools may be beautiful places in which children can learn to live and grow.

References

Ackerman, D. (1990). *A natural history of the senses.* New York: Random House.

Ahrentzen, S. B. (1988). Elementary education facilities. In *Encyclopedia of architecture design, engineering and construction* (Vol. 2, pp. 331-337). New York: John Wiley.

Alexander, T. M. (1987). *John Dewey's theory of art, experience and nature: The horizons of feeling.* Albany: State University of New York Press.

Anderson, C. W. (1990). *Pragmatic liberalism.* Chicago: University of Chicago Press.

Aper, J. P., & Garrison, J. W. (1989). Philosophy, science, and social inquiry: Contemporary methodological controversies in social science and related applied fields of research. *Educational Studies, 20*(1), 19-28.

Apple, M. (1982). *Education and power.* Boston: Routledge & Kegan Paul.

Applied Technology Research Corporation. (1992). *Restructuring schools: A research project sponsored by the State of Louisiana Department of Education.* Baton Rouge: Louisiana Department of Education.

Archbald, D. (1993). Restructuring in the eyes of practitioners: An analysis of "Next Century" school restructuring proposals. *International Journal of Educational Reform, 2*(4), 384-397.

Arendt, H. (1958). *The human condition.* Chicago: University of Chicago Press.

Bacon, F. (1899). *Advancement of learning and novum organum.* New York: Colonial.

Balbus, I. (1971). The concept of interest in pluralist and Marxian analysis. *Politics and Society, 1*(2), 154.

Barber, B. R. (1984). *Strong democracy: Participatory politics for a new age.* Berkeley: University of California Press.

Barber, B. R., & McGrath, M. J. G. (Eds.). (1982). *The artist and political vision.* New Brunswick, NJ: Transaction Books.

Barnard, C. I. (1938). *Functions of the executive.* Cambridge, MA: Harvard University Press.

182

Barzun, J. (1983). *A stroll with William James.* New York: Harper & Row.

Bates, R. J. (1980). Educational administration, sociology of knowledge and the management of knowledge. *Educational Administration Quarterly, 16*(2), 1-20.

Bates, R. J. (1987). Corporate culture, schooling, and educational administration. *Educational Administration Quarterly, 23*(4), 79-116.

Bateson, M. C. (1989). *Composing a life.* New York: Atlantic Monthly Press.

Baudrillard, J. (1993). *The transparency of evil* (J. Benedict, Trans.). London: Verso.

Beck, L. G. (1992). Meeting the challenge of the future: The place of a caring ethic in educational administration. *American Journal of Education, 100*(4), 454-496.

Beck, L. G. (1994). *Reclaiming educational administration as a caring profession.* New York: Teachers College Press.

Beck, L. G., & Newman, R. L. (1993, April). *Caring in the educational setting: Notes from the field.* Paper presented at the annual meeting of the American Educational Research Association, Atlanta, GA.

Bennett, W. J. (1993). *Book of virtues.* New York: Simon & Schuster.

Bentley, A. F. (1935). *Behavior knowledge fact.* Bloomington, IN: Principia.

Bentley, A. F. (1954). *Inquiry into inquiries: Essays in social theory* (S. Ratner, Ed., with an introduction). Boston: Beacon.

Bentley, A. F. (1967). *The process of government* (P. H. Odegard, Ed., with an introduction). Cambridge, MA: Harvard University Press. (Original work published 1908)

Bergquist, W. (1993). *The postmodern organization: Mastering the art of irreversible change.* San Francisco: Jossey-Bass.

Bernal, M. E., & Knight, G. P. (Eds.). (1993). *Ethnic identity.* Buffalo: State University of New York Press.

Bernstein, R. J. (1966). *John Dewey.* New York: Washington Square Press.

Bernstein, R. J. (1983). *Beyond objectivism and relativism: Science, hermeneutics, and praxis.* Philadelphia: University of Pennsylvania Press.

Bernstein, R. J. (1992). *The new constellation: The ethical-political horizons of modernity/postmodernity.* Cambridge, MA: MIT Press.

Bidwell, C. E. (1965). The school as a formal organization. In J. March (Ed.), *Handbook of organizations* (pp. 974-1022). Chicago: Rand McNally.

Bloom, A. (1987). *The closing of the American mind.* New York: Simon & Schuster.

Bode, B. H. (1937). *Democracy as a way of life.* New York: Macmillan.

Bode, B. H. (1938). *Progressive education at the crossroads.* New York: Newsom.

Bode, B. H. (1939). Ends and means in education, or, the conflicts in our cultural heritage. In B. H. Bode, J. Dewey, & T. V. Smith, *What is democracy?* Norman, OK: Cooperative Books.

Bolman, L. G., & Deal, T. E. (1991). *Reframing organizations: Artistry, choice, and leadership.* San Francisco: Jossey-Bass.

Bourdieu, P., & Passeron, J. (1977). *Reproduction in education, society and culture* (R. Nice, Trans.). London: Sage.

Bredo, E. (1989). Review article: After positivism, what? *Educational Theory, 39*(4), 401-413.

Bryk, A. S., Easton, J. Q., Kerbow, D., Rollow, S. G., & Sebring, P. A. (1994). The state of Chicago school reform. *Phi Delta Kappan, 76*(1), 74-78.

Burrell, G., & Morgan, G. (1979). *Sociological paradigms and organizational analysis.* Portsmouth, NH: Heinemann.

Callahan, R. (1962). *Education and the cult of efficiency.* Chicago: University of Chicago Press.

Campbell, J. (1992). *The community reconstructs: The meaning of pragmatic social thought.* Urbana: University of Illinois Press.

Capper, C. (Ed.). (1993). *Educational administration in a pluralistic society.* Albany: State University of New York Press.

Card, C. (1990). Caring and evil. *Hypatia, 5*(1), 100-108.

Carnoy, M., & Levin, H. M. (1976). *The limits of educational reform.* New York: David McKay.

Charters, W. W. (1925). *Personal leadership in industry.* New York: McGraw-Hill.

Cherryholmes, C. H. (1988). *Power and criticism: Poststructural investigations in education.* New York: Teachers College Press.

Chicago School Reform Act (P.A. 84-126), Ill. Rev. Stat. ch. 122, par. 34-1.01 et seq. (1989).

Childs, J. L. (1956). *American pragmatism and education.* New York: Henry Holt.

Childs, J. L. (1967). *Education and morals: An experimentalist philosophy of education.* New York: John Wiley. (Original work published 1950)

Chubb, J. E., & Moe, T. M. (1990). *Politics, markets, and America's schools.* Washington, DC: Brookings Institution.

Cibulka, J. G. (1975). School decentralization in Chicago. *Education and Urban Society, 7*(4), 412-438.

Clark, D. L., Astuto, T. A., Foster, W. P., Gaynor, A. K., & Hart, A. W. (1994). Taxonomy and overview. In W. K. Hoy (Ed.), *Domain III organizational studies, educational administration: The UCEA document base* (pp. 1-38). New York: McGraw-Hill.

Corbett, H., Dickson, H., Firestone, W. A., & Rossman, G. B. (1987). Resistance to planned change and the sacred in school cultures. *Educational Administration Quarterly, 23*(4), 36-59.

Cremin, L. A. (1961). *The transformation of the school.* New York: Random House.

Cremin, L. A. (1988). *American education: The metropolitan experience, 1876-1980.* New York: Harper & Row.

Crews, F. (1986, May 29). *The return of grand theory in the human sciences* edited by Quentin Skinner [Review]. *New York Review of Books,* p. 36.

Cusick, P. (1987). Organizational culture and schools. *Educational Administration Quarterly, 23*(4), 3-17.

Daume, D., & Pardo, E. (1993, November 16). Still not dealing with school funding. *Chicago Tribune.*

Deal, T. E., & Peterson, K. (1994). *The leadership paradox: Balancing logic and artistry in schools.* San Francisco: Jossey-Bass.

d'Entreves, M. P. (1989). Freedom, plurality, solidarity: Hannah Arendt's theory of action. *Philosophy and Social Criticism, 15*(4), 317-350.

Dewey, J. (1909). *Moral principles in education.* Carbondale: Southern Illinois University Press.

Dewey, J. (1915). *The school and society* (rev. ed.). Chicago: University of Chicago Press. (Original work published 1899)

Dewey, J. (1916a). *Democracy and education.* New York: Macmillan.

Dewey, J. (1916b). Nationalizing education. In *Addresses and proceedings of the fifty-fourth annual meeting, National Education Association* (pp. 183-189). Ann Arbor, MI: National Education Association.

Dewey, J. (1929). *The quest for certainty: A study of the relation of knowledge and action.* New York: G. P. Putnam's Sons.

Dewey, J. (1930). *Individualism, old and new.* New York: Minton, Balch.

Dewey, J. (1934). *Art as experience.* New York: Minton, Balch.

Dewey, J. (1935). *Liberalism and social action.* New York: G. P. Putnam's Sons.

Dewey, J. (1937). Democracy and educational administration. *School and Society, 45,* 457-462.

Dewey, J. (1938). *Logic: The theory of inquiry.* New York: Henry Holt.

Dewey, J. (1946). *The public and its problems.* Chicago: Gateway. (Original work published 1927)

Dewey, J. (1955). *The public and its problems.* Denver, CO: Alan Swallow. (Original work published 1927)

Dewey, J. (1958). *Experience and nature.* New York: Dover. (Original work published 1926)

Dewey, J., & Bentley, A. F. (1949). *Knowing and the known.* Boston: Beacon.

Diesing, P. (1991). *How does social science work?* Pittsburgh, PA: University of Pittsburgh Press.

Doll, W. E., Jr. (1993). *A post-modern perspective on curriculum.* New York: Teachers College Press.

Dryzek, J. S. (1990). *Discursive democracy: Politics, policy, and political science.* Cambridge, UK: Cambridge University Press.

Duke, D. L. (1986). Aesthetics of leadership. *Educational Administration Quarterly, 22*(1), 7-27.

Durkin, J. T. (1993, December 5). Voice of the people [Column]. *Chicago Tribune.*

Eisner, E. W. (1988). The primacy of experience and the politics of method. *Educational Researcher, 17*(5), 15-20.

Eisner, E. W. (1994). *The educational imagination: On the design and evaluation of school programs* (3rd ed.). New York: Macmillan. (Original work published 1979)

Ellsworth, E. (1989). Why doesn't this feel empowering? Working through the repressive myths of critical pedagogy. *Harvard Educational Review, 59*(3), 297-324.

Elmore, R. (1990). *Restructuring schools: The next generation of education reform.* San Francisco: Jossey-Bass.

English, F. (1994). *Discourse and theory in educational administration.* New York: HarperCollins.

Epps, E. G. (1994). Radical school reform in Chicago: How is it working? In C. E. Finn, Jr., & H. J. Walberg (Eds.), *Radical education reforms* (pp. 95-116). Berkeley, CA: McCutchan.

Evers, C. W., & Lakomski, G. (1991). *Knowing educational administration: Contemporary methodological controversies in educational administration research.* Oxford, UK: Pergamon.

Fantini, M. (1976). *Public schools of choice.* New York: Simon & Schuster.

Fay, B. (1987). *Critical social science: Liberation and its limits.* Ithaca, NY: Cornell University Press.

Fayol, H. (1949). *General and industrial management* (C. Storrs, Trans.). London: Pitman & Sons.

Fazzaro, C. J., Walter, J. E., & McKerrow, K. K. (1994). Education administration in a postmodern society: Implications for moral practice. In S. J. Maxcy (Ed.), *Postmodern school leadership: Meeting the crisis in educational administration* (pp. 85-95). Westport, CT: Praeger.

Fernandez, J. A., with J. Underwood (1993). *Tales out of school.* Boston: Little, Brown.

Fesmire, S. (1994, March 5). *Dewey and the moral artist.* Paper presented at the meeting of the Society for the Advancement of American Philosophy, Houston, TX.

Finn, C. (1991). *We must take charge: Our schools and our future.* New York: Free Press.

Firestone, W. A., & Wilson, B. L. (1985). Using bureaucratic and cultural linkages to improve instruction: The principal's contribution. *Educational Administration Quarterly, 21*(2), 7-31.

Follett, M. P. (1924). *Creative experience.* London: Longmans & Green.

Follett, M. P. (1942). *Dynamic administration* (H. C. Metcalf & L. Urwick, Eds.). New York: Harper.

Foster, W. (1986). *Paradigms and promises: New approaches to educational administration.* Buffalo, NY: Prometheus.

Foucault, M. (1972). *The archaeology of knowledge and the discourse on language* (A. M. S. Smith, Trans.). New York: Pantheon. (Original work published 1969)

Foucault, M. (1980). *Power/knowledge: Selected interviews and other writings, 1972-1977* (C. Gordon, Ed.; C. Gordon, L. Marshall, J. Mepham, & K. Soper, Trans.). New York: Pantheon.

Freire, P. (1970a). The adult literacy process in cultural action for freedom. *Harvard Educational Review, 40*(3), 205-225.

Freire, P. (1970b). Cultural action and conscientization. *Harvard Educational Review, 40*(3), 452-477.

Freire, P. (1970c). *Pedagogy of the oppressed* (M. B. Rames, Trans.). New York: Seabury.

Freire, P. (1973). *Education for critical consciousness.* New York: Seabury.

Freire, P. (1985). *The politics of education.* South Hadley, MA: Bergin & Garvey.

Freire, P., & Macedo, D. (1987). *Literacy: Reading the word and the world.* South Hadley, MA: Bergin & Garvey.

Fukuyama, F. (1992). *The end of history and the last man.* New York: Free Press.

Gilligan, C. (1982). *In a different voice: Psychological theory and women's development.* Cambridge, MA: Harvard University Press.

Giroux, H. A. (1983). *Theories and resistance in education.* South Hadley, MA: Bergin & Garvey.

Giroux, H. A. (1985). Critical pedagogy, cultural politics and the discourse of experience. *Journal of Education, 167*(2), 22-41.

Giroux, H. A. (1988a). Border pedagogy in the age of postmodernism. *Journal of Education, 170*(3), 162-181.

Giroux, H. A. (1988b). Postmodernism and the discourse of educational criticism. *Journal of Education, 170*(3), 5-30.

Giroux, H. A. (1988c). *Schooling and the struggle for public life: Critical pedagogy in the modern age.* Minneapolis: University of Minnesota Press.

Giroux, H. A. (1988d). *Teachers as intellectuals: Toward a critical pedagogy of learning.* Granby, MA: Bergin & Garvey.

Gitlin, A. T. (1965, September 3). Local pluralism as theory and ideology. *Studies on the Left,* pp. 21-45.

Gleick, J. (1987). *Chaos: Making a new science.* New York: Penguin.

Gordon, M. O. (1964). *Assimilation in American life.* New York: Oxford University Press.

Gould, C. (1988). *Rethinking democracy.* Cambridge, UK: Cambridge University Press.

Green, B., & Bigum, C. (1993). Governing chaos: Postmodern science, informational technology and educational administration. *Educational Philosophy and Theory, 2*(2), 79-103.

Griffiths, D., Hart, A. H., & Blair, B. G. (1991). Still another approach to administration: Chaos theory. *Educational Administration Quarterly, 27*(3), 430-451.

Gunts, E. (1993). Architecture for kids: A new design frontier challenges architects. *Architecture, 82*(4), 43-45.

Gutmann, A. (1987). *Democratic education.* Princeton, NJ: Princeton University Press.

Habermas, J. (1993). *Justification and application: Remarks on discourse ethics* (C. Cronin, Trans.). Cambridge, MA: MIT Press.

Hassard, J. (1991). Multiple paradigms and organizational analysis: A case study. *Organization Studies, 12*(2), 275-299.

Hayles, N. K. (1990). *Chaos bound: Orderly disorder in contemporary literature and science.* Ithaca, NY: Cornell University Press.

Heidegger, M. (1962). *Being and time* (J. Macquarrie & E. S. Robinson, Trans.). New York: Harper & Row. (Original work published 1927)

Hess, G. A., Jr. (1991). *School restructuring, Chicago style.* Newbury Park, CA: Corwin.

Hijuelos, O. (1989). *The mambo kings play songs of love.* Farrar, Straus, & Giroux.

Hirsch, E. D. (1987). *Cultural literacy: What every American needs to know.* Boston: Houghton Mifflin.

Hoagland, S. L. (1991). Some thoughts about "caring." In C. Card (Ed.), *Feminist ethics* (pp. 246-263). Lawrence: University of Kansas Press.

Hobbes, T. (1950). *Leviathan.* New York: Dutton.

Hodgkinson, C. (1991). *Educational leadership.* Albany: State University of New York Press.

Hofstadter, D. R. (1985). *Metamagical themas: Questing for the essence of mind and pattern.* New York: Basic Books.

Hook, S. (1939). *John Dewey.* New York: John Day.

Hoy, W. K., & Miskel, C. G. (1991). *Educational administration: Theory, research, and practice* (4th ed.). New York: McGraw-Hill.

Imber-Black, E., & Roberts, J. (1992). *Rituals for our times.* New York: HarperCollins.

Jackson, N., & Carter, P. (1991). In defense of paradigm incommensurability. *Organization Studies, 12*(1), 109-127.

Jackson, P. W., Boostrom, R. E., & Hansen, D. T. (1993). *The moral life of schools.* San Francisco: Jossey-Bass.

Jameson, F. (1991). *Postmodernism, or the cultural logic of late capitalism.* Durham, NC: Duke University Press.

Jencks, C. (1972). *Inequality: A reassessment of schooling in America.* New York: Anchor.

Jencks, C. (1979). *Who gets ahead: The determinants of economic success in America.* New York: Basic Books.

Johnston, B. J. (1994). Educational administration in the postmodern age. In S. J. Maxcy (Ed.), *Postmodern school leadership: Meeting the crisis in educational administration* (pp. 115-131). Westport, CT: Praeger.

Kallen, H. M. (1925). *Education, the machine and the worker.* New York: New Republic.

Kallen, H. M. (1956). *Cultural pluralism and the American idea.* Philadelphia: University of Pennsylvania Press.

Kallen, H. M. (1970). *Culture and democracy in the United States.* New York: Arno and the *New York Times.* (Original work published 1924)

Kaplan, A. (1958). *American ethics and public policy.* New York: Oxford University Press.

Katz, M. (1968). *The irony of early school reform.* Cambridge, MA: Harvard University Press.

Kentucky Department of Education. (1990). *Kentucky School Laws.* Frankfort, KY: Banks-Baldwin Law Publishing.

Kristeva, J. (1986). *The Kristeva reader.* New York: Columbia University Press.

Kuhn, T. S. (1970). *The structure of scientific revolutions* (2nd ed.). Chicago: University of Chicago Press. (Original work published 1962)

Lakatos, I. (1970). Falsification and the methodology of scientific research programmes. In I. Lakatos & A. Musgrave (Eds.), *Criticism and the growth of knowledge* (pp. 91-196). Cambridge, UK: Cambridge University Press.

Lasch, C. (1991). *The true and only heaven: Progress and its critics.* New York: Norton.

Lenson, D. (1987). *The birth of tragedy: A commentary.* Boston: Twayne.

Liston, D. (1988). Examining Marxist explanations of schools. *American Journal of Education, 96*(3), 323-350.

Lyotard, J. F. (1984). *The postmodern condition: A report on knowledge* (G. Bennington & B. Masumi, Trans.). Minneapolis: University of Minnesota Press.

MacIntyre, A. (1981). *After virtue.* Notre Dame, IN: University of Notre Dame Press.

March, J. G., & Olsen, J. P. (1976). *Ambiguity and choice in organizations.* Bergin, Norway: Universitetsforlaget.

Marion, R. (1992). Chaos, topology, and social organization. *Journal of School Leadership, 2,* 144-177.

Marshall, C. (1992). *The assistant principal: Leadership choices and challenges.* Newbury Park, CA: Corwin.

Maxcy, S. J. (1991). *Educational leadership: A critical pragmatic perspective.* New York: Bergin & Garvey.

Maxcy, S. J. (Ed.). (1994). *Postmodern school leadership: Meeting the crisis in educational administration.* Westport, CT: Praeger.

Maxcy, S. J., & Maxcy, D. O. (1992). Design, leadership and higher education. In J. J. Van Patten (Ed.), *Academic profiles in higher education* (pp. 329-351). Lewiston, NY: Edwin Mellen.

Maxwell, J. (1992). Understanding and validity in qualitative research. *Harvard Educational Review, 62*(3), 279-300.

Maxwell, N. (1984). *From knowledge to wisdom.* Oxford, UK: Basil Blackwell.

Mayo, E. (1933). *The human problems of an industrial civilization.* Boston: Harvard Business School.

McKinney, J. R., & Garrison, J. W. (1994). Postmodernism and educational leadership: The new and improved panopticon. In S. J. Maxcy (Ed.), *Postmodern school leadership: Meeting the crisis in educational administration* (pp. 71-83). Westport, CT: Praeger.

McLaren, P. (1993). *Schooling as ritual performance* (2nd ed.). New York: Routledge.

McLaren, P. (1994). Multiculturalism and the post-modern critique: Toward a pedagogy of resistance and transformation. In H. A. Giroux & P. McLaren (Eds.), *Between borders: Pedagogy and the politics of cultural studies* (pp. 192-222). New York: Routledge.

Michels, R. (1959). *Political parties.* New York: Dover.

Miron, L., & Elliott, R. J. (1994). Moral leadership in a poststructural era. In S. J. Maxcy (Ed.), *Postmodern school leadership: Meeting the crisis in educational administration* (pp. 133-140). Westport, CT: Praeger.

Morgan, G. (1986). *Images of organization.* Beverly Hills, CA: Sage.

Murphy, J. (1991). *Restructuring schools: Capturing and assessing the phenomena.* New York: Teachers College Press.

Murphy, J. (1993). *The landscape of leadership preparation: Reframing the education of school administrators.* Newbury Park, CA: Corwin.

National Commission on Excellence in Education. (1983). *A nation at risk: The imperative for education reform*. Washington, DC: Government Printing Office.

Nietzsche, F. W. (1949). *Beyond good and evil*. Chicago: Regnery.

Nietzsche, F. W. (1956). *The birth of tragedy and the genealogy of morals*. Garden City, NY: Doubleday.

Nietzsche, F. W. (1967). *Thus spake Zarathustra* (T. Common, Trans.). New York: Heritage.

Noblit, G. (1993, April). *Instituting caring in a school: Principal contradictions*. Paper presented at the annual meeting of the American Educational Research Association, Atlanta, GA.

Noddings, N. (1984). *Caring: A feminine approach to ethics and moral education*. Berkeley: University of California Press.

Oakes, J. (1985). *Keeping track: How schools structure inequality*. New Haven, CT: Yale University Press.

Oliver, D. W., with Gershman, K. W. (1989). *Education, modernity, and fractured meaning: Toward a process theory of teaching and learning*. Albany: State University of New York Press.

Parker, M., & McHugh, G. (1991). Five texts in search of an author: A response to John Hassard's "Multiple paradigms and organizational analysis." *Organization Studies, 12*(3), 451-456.

Peirce, C. S. (1963a). *Collected papers of Charles Sanders Peirce: Vol. 5. Pragmatism and pragmaticism* (C. Hartshorne & P. Weiss, Eds.) (pp. 47-54). Cambridge, MA: Belknap/Harvard University Press. (Original work published 1934)

Peirce, C. S. (1963b). *Collected papers of Charles Sanders Peirce: Vol. 6. Scientific metaphysics* (C. Hartshorne & P. Weiss, Eds.). Cambridge, MA: Belknap/Harvard University Press. (Original work published 1934)

Perkinson, H. J. (1991). *The imperfect panacea: American faith in education 1865-1990* (3rd ed.). New York: McGraw-Hill.

Perry, R. B. (Ed.). (1922). *Essays in radical empiricism by William James*. New York: Longmans & Green.

Peters, T. (1987). *Thriving on chaos*. New York: HarperCollins.

Peters, T. (1992). *Liberation management*. New York: Norton.

Peterson, P. E. (1985). *The politics of school reform 1870-1940*. Chicago: University of Chicago Press.

Phillips, D. C. (1987). *Philosophy, science and social inquiry*. Oxford, UK: Pergamon.

Pohland, P. A. (1992). Paradigm and prospect: Educational administration and reform. *UCEA Review, 33*(2), 4-14.

Popkewitz, T. S. (1984). *Paradigm and ideology in educational research: The social functions of the intellectual*. London: Falmer.

Poster, M. (Ed.). (1988). *Jean Baudrillard: Selected writings*. Cambridge, UK: Polity.

Power, F. C. (1993). Just schools and moral atmosphere. In K. A. Strike & P. L. Ternasky (Eds.), *Ethics for professionals in education: Perspectives for preparation and practice* (pp. 148-161). New York: Teachers College Press.

Priesmeyer, H. R. (1992). *Organizations and chaos: Defining the methods of nonlinear management*. Westport, CT: Quorum.

Prigogine, I., & Stengers, I. (1984). *Order out of chaos: Man's new dialogue with nature*. Toronto: Bantam New Age.

Purpel, D. E. (1989). *The moral and spiritual crisis in education*. Granby, MA: Bergin & Garvey.

Putnam, H., & Putnam, R. A. (1993). Education for democracy. *Educational theory,* 43(4), 361-376.

Quantz, R. A., & McCabe, N. C. (1991). Continuing the conversation: A response to Apple, Johnston, and Sergiovanni. *Urban Review, 23*(1), 51-57.

Raup, R.B.G., Axtelle, G., Benne, K., & Smith, B. O. (1950). *The improvement of practical intelligence.* New York: Harper & Brothers. (Original work published 1943)

Ravitch, D. (1983). *The troubled crusade: American education 1945-1980.* New York: Basic Books.

Reyes, P. (1993). Cultural citizenship and social responsibility: A call for change in educational administration [Presidential address presented at the annual meeting of the University Council for Educational Administration]. *UCEA Review, 25*(1), 1, 11-13.

Roethlisberger, F. J., & Dickson, W. J. (1939). *Management and the worker.* Cambridge, MA: Harvard University Press.

Rorty, R. J. (1979). *Philosophy and the mirror of nature.* Princeton, NJ: Princeton University Press.

Rorty, R. J. (1983). *The consequences of pragmatism: Essays 1972-1980.* Minneapolis: University of Minnesota Press.

Rorty, R. J. (1985). Solidarity or objectivity? In J. Rajehman & C. West (Eds.), *Post-analytic philosophy* (p. 16). New York: Columbia University Press.

Rorty, R. J. (1989). *Contingency, irony, and solidarity.* Cambridge, UK: Cambridge University Press.

Rorty, R. J. (1991). *Objectivity, relativism, and truth: Philosophical papers* (Vol. 1). Cambridge, UK: Cambridge University Press.

Rose v. The Council for Better Education, Inc. (Supreme Court of Kentucky), 790 S.W.2d 186 (1989).

Rosenau, P. M. (1992). *Postmodernism and the social sciences: Insights, inroads, and intrusions.* Princeton, NJ: Princeton University Press.

Rosenthal, S. B. (1986). *Speculative pragmatism.* Amherst: University of Massachusetts Press.

Rouse, J. (1987). *Knowledge and power: Toward a political philosophy of science.* Ithaca, NY: Cornell University Press.

Scheurich, J. J. (1994). Social relativism: A postmodernist epistemology for educational administration. In S. J. Maxcy (Ed.), *Postmodern school leadership: Meeting the crisis in educational administration* (pp. 17-46). Westport, CT: Praeger.

Sergiovanni, T. J. (1992). *Moral leadership: Getting to the heart of school improvement.* San Francisco: Jossey-Bass.

Sheridan, A. (1980). *Foucault: The will to truth.* London: Tavistock.

Shlain, L. (1991). *Art and physics: Parallel visions in space, time, and light.* New York: William Morrow.

Shor, I. (1987). *Critical teaching for everyday life.* Chicago: University of Chicago Press. (Original work published 1980)

Shor, I. (1992). *Empowering education: Critical teaching for social change.* Chicago: University of Chicago Press.

Shotter, J. (1993). *Cultural politics of everyday life.* Toronto: University of Toronto Press.

Simon, H. (1965). *Administrative behavior: A study of the decision-making processes in administrative organization* (2nd ed.). New York: Free Press. (Original work published 1947)

Simon, H. (1971). *The sciences of the artificial.* Cambridge, MA: MIT Press.

Sleeper, R. W. (1986). *The necessity of pragmatism: John Dewey's conception of philosophy.* New Haven, CT: Yale University Press.

Sleeter, C. E., & Grant, C. A. (1985). Race, class, and gender in an urban school: A case study. *Urban Education, 20*(1), 37-60.

Smelser, N. J. (1992). Culture: Coherent or incoherent. In R. Münch & N. J. Smelser (Eds.), *Theory of culture* (pp. 3-28). Berkeley: University of California Press.

Smiley, M. (1992). *Moral responsibility and the boundaries of community.* Chicago: University of Chicago Press.

Snauwaert, D. T. (1993). *Democracy, education, and governance: A developmental conception.* Buffalo: State University of New York Press.

Stanley, W. B. (1992). *Curriculum for utopia: Social reconstructionism and critical pedagogy in the postmodern era.* Albany: State University of New York Press.

Steffy, B. E. (1993a). *The Kentucky educational reform: Lessons for America.* Lancaster, PA: Technomic.

Steffy, B. E. (1993b, September). Top-down—Bottom-up: Systematic change in Kentucky. *Educational Leadership,* pp. 42-44.

Steffy, B. E., & English, F. W. (1994). Wildcard educational reform in Kentucky. In C. E. Finn, Jr., & H. J. Walberg (Eds.), *Radical education reforms* [National Society for the Study of Education Yearbook] (pp. 51-74). Berkeley, CA: McCutchan.

Stewart, I., & Golubitsky, M. (1992). *Fearful symmetry: Is god a geometer?* Oxford, UK: Blackwell.

Sungaila, H. (1990). Organizations alive: Have we at last found the key to a science of educational administration? *Studies in Educational Administration, 52,* 3-26.

Taylor, C. (1989). *Sources of the self.* Cambridge, MA: Harvard University Press.

Taylor, D. & Teddlie, C. (1992, April). *Restructuring and the classroom: A view from a reform district.* Paper presented at the annual meeting of the American Educational Research Association, San Francisco.

Taylor, F. W. (1911). *The principals of scientific management.* New York: Harper & Row.

Teachers feel left out of reform. (1993, September 1). *New York Times.*

Toulmin, S. (1990). *Cosmopolis.* New York: Free Press.

Trueba, H. T. (1993). Race and ethnicity: The role of universities in healing multicultural America. *Educational Theory, 43*(1), 41-54.

Tyack, D. (1974). *The one best system: A history of American urban education.* Cambridge, MA: Harvard University Press.

Tyack, D. (1990). Restructuring in historical perspective: Tinkering toward utopia. *Teachers College Record, 92*(2), 170-190.

Warren, R. P. (1946). *All the king's men.* New York: Harcourt, Brace.

Webb, R., Bondy, E., & Rose, D. (1994, April). *Governance and leadership dilemmas in restructured schools.* Paper presented at the annual meeting of the American Educational Research Association, New Orleans, LA.

Weick, K. (1976). Educational organizations as loosely coupled systems. *Administrative Science Quarterly, 21*(1), 1-19.

West, C. (1989). *The American evasion of philosophy: A genealogy of pragmatism.* Madison: University of Wisconsin Press.

West, C. (1993). *Keeping faith: Philosophy and race in America.* New York: Routledge.

Westbrook, R. B. (1991). *John Dewey and American democracy.* Ithaca, NY: Cornell University Press.

Willis, P. (1977). *Learning to labor.* Westmead, UK: Saxon House.

Willis, W. (1991). Education reform in Kentucky: A moral dilemma. In W. Willis (Ed.), *Proceedings of the forty-first annual meeting of the Philosophy of Education Society* (pp. 119-123). Morehead, KY: Morehead State University.

Wittgenstein, L. (1953). *Philosophical investigations* (G. E. M. Anscombe & R. Rhees, Eds.). Oxford, UK: Blackwell.

Wolff, R. P. (1969). *A critique of pure tolerance.* Boston: Beacon.

Zangwill, I. (1914). *The melting pot: Drama in four acts.* New York: Macmillan.

Zeitlin, I. M. (1968). *Ideology and the development of sociological theory.* Englewood Cliffs, NJ: Prentice Hall.

Index